By opening and using the chakras, one becomes able to be senior to the body and use it for one's spiritual purpose. As you "open the seal" of each chakra, you discover what you have to work with, what you need to let go of, what your purpose is in this life and how to complete your goals.

It is recommended that you read the Key series in the following order:

Meditation: *Key to Spiritual Awakening*

Healing: *Key to Spiritual Balance*

Clairvoyance: *Key to Spiritual Perspective*

Chakras: *Key to Spiritual Opening*

Each spiritual textbook gives a foundation in basic techniques which help you gain a spiritual awareness necessary for the use of the information that follows. All of the material is of a spiritual nature. Allow a spiritual perspective and you will benefit from the information. You must practice the techniques for them to work for you because you cannot intellectualize spiritual information.

CHAKRAS

Key to Spiritual Opening

by Mary Ellen Flora

CDM Publications • Everett, Washington

Art: Gail Coupal

Cover: Gail Coupal

Requests for such permission should be addressed to:

CDM Publications

2402 Summit Ave.

Everett, WA 98201

First Printing 1993

Printed in the United States of America

Library of Congress Catalog Card Number: 93-73958

ISBN 0-9631993-6-6

To Doc, with love.

ACKNOWLEDGEMENTS

There are many people who have helped with the creation of this book. Most of them do not know how important they have been in helping me. So thank you to Maris Gibson, my masseuse, Charlie Phillips, the survivor, Hannah Fitzgerald, the encourager, Marie Senestraro, Joan Mayshark, Sindi Somers, Deb Martin, and all those who have helped in so many ways.

Special thanks to Alison Eckels for her patient editorial work and her support and encouragement. Gail Coupal again blessed us with her artistic talents as a great favor to me and to all of us.

Thanks also to Reggie Taschereau for his careful proofreading, and to Michelle Guilford for her photographic talent. Also thanks to Jeff Gibson for his artistic advice and assistance.

I am most appreciative of the many ways Bill Broomall has helped to create this book with graphics, layout, organization, and many other things. Also, thank you to Bill for his song "Seven Wheels".

Love and thanks go also to my husband, Doc Slusher, for his support and encouragement.

TABLE OF CONTENTS

LIST OF ILLUSTRATIONS

SEVEN

SEALS

CHAKRAS

Key to Spiritual Opening

INTRODUCTION

An introduction to the chakra system is something I do with respect and reverence. You are spirit and a part of God. Your body is your vessel. The chakra system is the way you store and project your spiritual information in the physical world. Activating and using the chakras requires discipline, patience and a spiritual perspective. It is not something to be undertaken as a fad or temporary pursuit. Consciously activating the chakras is a lifelong journey. It is the ultimate in self-discovery. You must be prepared to meet yourself and all of your creations: the ones you like and the ones you do not like. Opening your chakras is opening the "book of you." Reading the book you have written and learning how to manifest it or change it is a great spiritual adventure.

Spiritual techniques are presented first to help you with the development of patience and the practice of discipline. These techniques help you focus your attention on your spiritual experience while staying in contact with your physical reality. By using the techniques you can activate your chakras in a safe and controlled manner. After an introduction of the basic principles, the chakra information is presented. Chakras are energy centers that contain our spiritual information. The techniques help cleanse and activate the chakras to make it easier to retrieve your information.

I have worked with my own chakra system for most of my life. Sometimes I have been aware of working with my chakras and other times I have not. For the past sixteen years I have taught others to use their chakras in a conscious manner. I have discovered that the unaware state is filled with problems, setbacks and disappointments that are not necessary. By being aware one can take greater control of any situation and make the path easier and more pleasant.

When I was twelve I broke my arm at the elbow. After the cast was removed, one night when I was half awake I looked at my elbow. I saw a brilliant wheel of light at the joint of my arm. There are chakras at all of the joints. I did not consciously know this at the time so at first I was afraid. I eventually relaxed and enjoyed the show of lights as if I were at a circus watching a Ferris wheel. It was clear to me that other people did not have experiences like this or did not talk about them, so I hid my new awareness inside myself. Even though I hid this experience for many years, it was indeed an awakening to myself as spirit.

When we go through life in an aware state, we can see that our changes are manifestations of our spiritual healing. Healing occurs when we open and consciously use the chakras. One student, who was training to be a teacher, experienced a great deal of competition with others during a particular growth process. She first judged her experience, since she believed that a soul with her training and practice should not be experiencing so much physical disturbance. She asked for spiritual assistance and with help she was able to see that she had opened her third chakra when she started her teaching program. This chakra contains information on how to distribute energy. She found that she had learned from her mother about the need to compete to get what she wanted in the world.

The student quickly realized she had to cleanse her mother's information from her third chakra so she could access her own information about how to manifest her power in the world. The information was correct for the mother but not for the daughter. When the student regained her own energy, she discovered a past life experience she needed to clear: a lifetime where she had been so competitive she had sabotaged her spiritual mission. She created the interaction with her mother in this life to help her discover her past mistake and clear it. Once she had cleared the past and the foreign energies, she found her own way of relating to power and distributing her energies.

Opening the chakras allows a great deal of personal discovery. We have to be prepared to see what we like and what we do not like about ourselves. We need to let go of judgement about our interactions with others to allow healing to occur. The cleansing and healing are necessary for the free motion of each chakra and the full access and use of the information it contains.

You might think of a chakra like a compact disk in a CD player. If the compact disk is not turning, the system is blocked and you cannot retrieve the information. When you discover the interference and correct it, the disk moves freely and the system is restored to full function. Surely, you would not judge an electrical malfunction in a CD player. Foreign energy or a past mistake is like the malfunction and needs to be released with as little fuss as you would create when you repair the compact disk player.

Another student experienced the need for self-forgiveness when he began to clear his second chakra. This chakra contains emotional and sexual information. He discovered a great deal of pain that he had created in his relationships with women. He had been hurt in two relationships where his partners had been unfaithful to him. This was difficult for him to comprehend intellectually, as he was faithful and loving to his partners. When he cleared the pain he had stored, he found a past life where he had been a very arrogant man who had no consideration for his partners. As he cleared the past life experience he was able to stop creating painful relationships in the present. He had been punishing himself for past mistakes, rather than forgiving himself and moving along on his path.

Each individual will find a cornucopia of information in every chakra. There is both useful and inappropriate information in each chakra. We need to identify which is which and clear the past, the foreign and the disruptive energy so we can get to what is beneficial and useful. We have to clear what is not appropriate so we can access the information we need to fulfill our purpose in this life.

There is no correct order in which to open the chakras. Each individual has his or her own game plan and needs to follow it. The secret is to persevere and clear the doubt so you will continue the process through the difficult times. Just as with physical exercise, in meditation or self-healing there are easy and difficult periods and times when there seems to be no change. If you keep working with yourself, the results will come.

Even when you feel you are not progressing, there are subtle changes taking place.

The purpose of becoming aware of and opening your chakras is to know yourself and your God. It is necessary to know yourself in order to know God. Your path to God is through you. Your body and energy system are your personal means for communication and creation. As you create your life, you either open or close your communication with God. When you act, think and live in a beneficial manner, your communication opens. When you create hate, fear and doubt, your communication closes. Learning to access the information in your chakras helps you know yourself. You can then know how to live a life which manifests your communication and relationship with God.

A meditation student told the story of her friend's three year old son insisting on seeing his new baby sister alone. The parents were concerned that he might harm the newborn and they put him off. He continued to insist on seeing his sister alone, so after two weeks of his persistence, they allowed him to visit her without their supervision. They had a baby monitor in her room and listened during the visit to make sure the baby was safe. What they heard changed their view of life.

Their son entered the room and closed the door. He approached the crib and quietly asked his sister, "Tell me what it's like being with God. I'm beginning to forget." There was silence for about five minutes. Their son left the room and closed the door. He was satisfied after that and to his parents appeared much happier.

If at three years of age a child is forgetting God, how much have the rest of us forgotten? We all need to return our attention to God. We need to return our awareness to our Source and Goal, as the child did, and we too can regain a happier state. Through meditation and opening our spiritual information system we can consciously focus our attention back on God both within and around us.

The ultimate goal of all souls is reunion with God. Other experiences are lessons to help us mature enough to accomplish this purpose. If you learn to know yourself with the goal of knowing God, you will find great satisfaction. By living what you know of God to the best of your ability you will accomplish your purpose.

LESSONS TO LEARN

Everyone is spirit and is seeking his or her own way to return to the Godforce. Each of us is looking for or has found our unique contribution and our unique way to manifest ourselves as spirit. Regardless of the level of our development, we must eventually open our chakra system and see what we have written there. During this opening there will be both celebration and sadness. We will discover things we have collected and stored that we want to enhance and use more, and we will discover things we do not wish to keep. Great beauty and power will be part of what we find as we recognize that we are part of God. We will also have to face the mistakes we have made and forgive ourselves for them. We can cleanse and heal whatever we need to change so we can focus on what is beautiful in us.

We write our spiritual story with the concepts, pictures, symbols and formulas we have developed and collected as spirit throughout many lives. As spirit, we manifest through the vibration of our experiences and beliefs. Some of these creations we wish to avoid reviewing because we judge them. We do not want to accept the times we have been doubtful, afraid, jealous, greedy, or lustful, and done things we deem evil. So we begin to hide the hate, fear, guilt and grief, rather than bringing them into the light and clearing them from ourselves. All we have to do is accept what we have created and forgive ourselves for our times of weakness, and we can move on to greater strength. When we learn to accept ourselves as we are, we can change and grow to maturity. By letting go of fear, we release hate and have room for love. As we learn to love ourselves, we can learn to love others. When we clear the things we do not like, we allow the things we like to shine out. By washing the dirt from a window we can see the view outside and the light within.

Most people have more difficulty accepting how powerful, beautiful and loving they are as spirit than they have accepting their mistakes and faults. Most of the time we block ourselves from giving and receiving the love that is available to all of us. Instead, we create blocks to this love with our doubt, pain, fear and hate. We see ourselves as bodies rather than as spirit. We can clear the blocks by learning our spiritual lessons and moving beyond the illusion that we are only bodies. We can see that our experiences, even the most painful ones, are opportunities to learn and grow. When we heal ourselves, our spiritual beauty and light shine out.

We are immortal spirit and a part of God, the Creator of All Things. This association makes us a great deal more than most people believe they are. By letting go of the illusion that we are only a body, we open our awareness to the reality that we are spirit. By accepting ourselves as a part of God, we change everything in our lives. We can then see ourselves and others as immortal spirit and live our lives accordingly. This awakening stirs the desire to open the information that we have stored as spirit. A great deal of this wealth of spiritual information is located in the chakras.

Each soul has been given free will to make its own choices and create its own reality. We choose our parents, our way of life, our gender, how we will die and every aspect of our existence on this Earth. During each moment of life we choose what we will think, do, relate to, not do and so forth. Each action and thought is recorded for our future reference and as a display of who we are. We have this freedom of choice before and during each life so that we can choose God of our own free will. Only when we choose our path freely, without coercion, will we get where we are going. We travel through many stages of growth to mature enough to choose to return to God. The process involves learning to have all of our abilities and the wisdom and strength to return them to God. This does not happen in one life. There are many lives and many opportunities to learn what we need to know.

Reincarnation, or the experience of life in many different bodies, is one way we learn our lessons. We create through time and space while in bodies. Therefore, we need to understand how bodies work and how to bring our spiritual energy into our body. The lessons about how to operate a body often require several lives. The lessons about how to master the chakra system take more lives than most of us have lived. We may take several lives to achieve mastery over one chakra.

By opening and using the chakras, one becomes able to be senior to one's body and use it for one's spiritual purpose. Consciously working with the chakra system is an exercise in gaining seniority with the physical body and the physical world. This work is necessary to gain the spiritual communication and mastery to return to the Godforce. Spiritual seniority is essential since the physical body is a powerful creation and one in which we have invested a great deal of energy. Most people allow the body to be senior and create their lives from the body's desires. By using the spiritual information in the chakras, one becomes aware of one's spiritual self and purpose. As a soul gains control of the chakras, he also gains greater control over his creativity and communication.

An example of this process is a person who is in a body to learn about power. She could begin her life operating from the illusion that the body is the total reality as her parents and society taught her this belief. By creating through this belief she would experience many power struggles in her life. She would create conflict in her work or home, and feel she had to fight or compete for whatever she wanted. During the life, as she matured and began to let go of other people's beliefs, she could rediscover her spiritual awareness. This would lead her to an awakened state of tuning in to her third chakra and beginning to distribute her energies in her own creative pattern. As she used her power in her unique spiritual way, she would learn her lessons with less struggle and greater pleasure.

It is possible to get an overview of our life to see what our main lesson is. We can look at each interaction and experience in terms of learning something spiritually. By discovering which chakra we are learning about, we can focus our attention and enhance our progress. We can learn to emphasize the information in one chakra and minimize the use of another. For example, we can learn to use our neutrality and be in charge of our emotions. By learning to use our chakras, we create more fully as spirit and are less controlled by the body and outside influences.

We need to learn to be senior to the body to create what we want as spirit. Most of the world is lost in greed, hate, fear and other destructive physical modes. We have millions of bodies creating in our world and not many of them are directed by the spiritual beings responsible for them. The beings are not taking responsibility for their bodies and learning how to use them properly, so the bodies are running the show. Much of this show is not pleasant, filled with the scenes of famine, war, greed, abuse and planetary destruction. All of this can change by each soul taking responsibility for its own body and what it creates through the body.

The chakra system is what we use to manifest ourselves as spirit. If this system is dormant, uncontrolled or improperly used, then the physical body, the ego or some outside influence is likely to be creating the life experience, rather than the soul creating its life according to its purpose. It is disturbing to realize how many souls are not in charge of their bodies and their lives. To take back control of the body and the lifetime, one only needs to focus on oneself as spirit. With this spiritual focus the chakra system begins to open and the information becomes accessible. Meditation is the easiest and safest way to create this spiritual awakening.

As we begin meditating and healing ourselves, we often focus first on the information we have accepted from others: the foreign energy and concepts in our system. While we must clear this foreign energy as part of our healing process and spiritual development, we must also learn to be senior to our own body for this cleansing process to work. When we own the body and energy system we have created, it is easy to clear the inappropriate energy. If we do not take responsibility for our body and system, we will just fill it with a different form of foreign energy when we clear the old.

Do not make the mistake of believing you have to literally walk on water or perform other amazing physical manifestations to confirm your spiritual seniority. You only need to take charge of your system so you, spirit, are the one creating your reality. This can bring you great satisfaction as you can find new meaning to your life when you create it as spirit. Taking responsibility for your body and taking control of your chakras is what you are meant to do. It allows you to lead a creative life in which you can develop your communication with your spiritual self and with your God.

As you "open the seal" of each chakra, you discover what you have to work with, what you need to let go of, what your purpose is in this life and how to complete your goals. You will also experience temptations. This is when you need your spiritual techniques to help you stay on your spiritual path. Many souls have progressed far and then lost their way on a temptation. It is necessary to maintain your spiritual focus to avoid these detours.

As you work with your chakras you will find many things you wish to clear. When you clear the old, it is necessary to own the newly created space with your spiritual energy. The following techniques will help you do these things and avoid or more easily navigate some of the temptations you will encounter. Temptations are a certainty, as part of being in a body is learning to be senior to that body and senior to the physical world. The more information you gain and the more power you have, the greater the temptations are to stray from your original purpose. As long as you are in a body you will encounter temptation.

You will encounter temptation as you open and continue to use your chakras. If you seek power, wealth, or any physical reward as your goal, you are already entwined with temptation. Enjoy the lessons without judgement and you will eventually master your challenges. Have faith and you can overcome the temptations. See opening the seals or chakras as an adventure and you will create an exciting lifelong journey.

Any time during the reading of this information you may find it helpful to meditate on what you have read. It is important to be clear on what is your truth and how you can use the information in your own life. You can do this by sitting quietly on a chair with your hands and feet separated, closing your eyes and focusing your awareness into the center of your head behind your eyes. You can then create an energy flow or cord from your first chakra, near the base of your spine, to the center of the Earth. By centering in the neutral place in your head and creating a connection with this reality to allow a safe communication between you and your body, you create a conscious space to see your own truth. Without this quiet time you can get confused by others' information and allow it to cloud your personal view.

It is essential to use some form of spiritual discipline when learning about the chakras. If you do not focus spiritually, it is dangerous as you will misunderstand or misuse the information. You may even be detoured completely from your original spiritual goals onto a physical sidetrack. If you focus only on the physical aspects, your experience will at best be just an intellectual exercise or at worst the misuse of a lifetime. Your spiritual focus could be as simple as personal faith in God or as involved as a life devoted to meditation and prayer. You are safe in your development as long as you stay tuned in to yourself as spirit and to your God. The techniques help you do this by helping you focus back on yourself as spirit.

Meditation is the safest way through your difficulties, and it will help you find beauty within yourself. As a part of God you have great beauty, joy and enthusiasm. You can let your light shine and continue to let it shine until you melt through the bushel you have placed on yourself. Every light that shines brings that much more light into the world.

Your lessons are not all unpleasant or difficult ones. Many of your lessons can be fun and joyous if you let them be. You are always your own worst enemy or your own best friend. Spiritual awareness helps you to be your best friend. It is in your power to be happy or unhappy. You can be in control of your life, happy with your creations and aware of what you are doing and where you are going. When you allow yourself to have your spiritual awareness, learning your lessons is easier and a lot more pleasant. The chakra system contains much of the information you need to be spiritually aware, and opening the chakras is one of your lessons.

Often you will find beliefs that cause you to struggle and fight against your changes and growth. It is helpful to learn not to resist yourself or your God. When you find judgement of your creations, and your guilt or shame stop your progress, use the techniques to regain your spiritual perspective and amusement. It is necessary to move above the body energies of guilt, grief, shame and so forth to respond to your spiritual self.

You change as you open and get to know yourself. By not resisting the changes you make, your progress is smooth. If you fight or resist the changes, your path will be bumpy and confusing. You will be fighting yourself instead of being open to your healing and growth. The techniques help you to be less resistant to change. Since your body likes things as they are, you will need to be aware of its resistance to change and learn to work with it to assist the healing process. Spiritual techniques help you learn to communicate with your body and work with it effectively. You need patience to create in the physical realm.

Together with God, you have created a life plan. By opening your spiritual centers and learning to know yourself as spirit, you discover this plan and learn how to follow it. As you follow the plan without resistance and without many detours, you arrive at your relationship with God and accomplish your life goals. Do not be afraid to make mistakes. Everyone makes mistakes. You have time to rectify your mistakes as you have many lives to learn your lessons. If you keep your spiritual focus as much as possible, the path is easier. The lessons are more fun to learn when you know you are spirit returning to God.

ꙅPIꙆITUAL TECHNIQUEꙅ

The best known and simplest chakra adjustment is the Lord's Prayer taught to us by Jesus Christ. This prayer contains key words that activate and adjust each chakra in present time. You can adjust your chakras by saying this prayer. When you combine this powerful prayer with the following meditation techniques, you create a dynamic healing energy.

The techniques presented can help you discover what you have stored in your chakras. They can assist you as you open and access the information in your chakras. By using these techniques you create a safe learning space for yourself. They also help you focus spiritually so your body, ego or external influences do not take charge and stop you. Your body can come up with amazing excuses that distract you from your purpose. The techniques help you focus spiritually so you can overcome any interference or distraction.

The techniques are: grounding, running earth and cosmic energies, gold energy, being in the center of your head, using a rose symbol, creating and destroying as spirit, awareness and control of the aura, and present time. These techniques will be used to get in touch with each of the seven major chakras. By using the techniques you can learn how to cleanse the chakras, how to identify foreign energy and clear it, how to focus your spiritual attention where you want it, and more.

Use the spiritual techniques to help you be in touch with yourself as spirit and with God. Your inner voice and the spiritual guidance you discover through use of the techniques will lead you to your goal. Your physical body is the vehicle through which you create and communicate in this world. The techniques will help you learn to be senior to your body and to use it for your benefit. Since bodies operate through time, it will take time for you to gain what you seek. Be patient and persevere and you will experience change in your life.

When your body or inappropriate beliefs get in your way, be patient with yourself. Use the techniques to turn within and to regain your spiritual perspective so you can clear the blocks and temptations. This process may take months in some situations and only moments in others. Validate what you accomplish rather than berating yourself when you stumble or fall. Learning to love yourself is part of the process.

You will discover and rediscover the importance of not resisting and of letting go of fear. You will resist and be afraid because you are in a body and that will be part of its experience. As you persevere, you will learn to let go and rejoice in your changes rather than fighting them. In the Bible the angels were constantly telling people, "fear not", "do not be afraid." They were reassuring us of God's presence and loving guidance. Even the great prophets and spiritual teachers had to be reminded of the need to let go and have faith. They had bodies just as we do.

The techniques presented can help you, guide you and give you something to hold onto that you can return to repeatedly to regain your balance. They are your safety connection, your focal point, your reminder that you are spirit and that your information needs to come from your spiritual self and your communication with God within. The techniques help you to not be afraid and to not resist so your growth can be easy and light.

To best experience the techniques, have a quiet place where you can be alone and undisturbed. Sit in a straight-backed chair with your spine as straight as possible. The straightness of your spine helps your energy flow smoothly. Put your feet flat on the floor and your hands in your lap. Keep your hands and feet separated to allow for a free flow of your energy. Close your eyes and turn your attention inward. Take a few deep breaths to relax your body and help the movement of your energy.

Use this basic format with each technique and with your meditation. The discipline of the posture helps you concentrate and allows your energy to flow smoothly. The breathing helps you relax your body and move your energy. Relax and enjoy your healing meditation.

◌ჳ The Lord's Prayer ℘

Our Father, Who art in Heaven, hallowed be Thy Name. Thy Kingdom come, Thy will be done, on Earth as it is in Heaven. Give us this day our daily bread, and forgive us our trespasses, as we forgive those who trespass against us. Keep us from temptation, and deliver us from evil. For Thine is the Kingdom, the Power, and the Glory forever, Amen.

GROUNDING AND
RELEASING ENERGY

Grounding is the foundation of the spiritual techniques. It helps you connect yourself to your body, and you and your body to the planet. With this connection you can be aware both of yourself as spirit and of your body and physical creations. Your ability to use the other techniques is dependent on your ability to ground. The more capable you are at grounding, the more you can manifest yourself as spirit in your body and in the world.

Grounding makes your body safe as you bring more spiritual energy into it. Grounding keeps your body secure as you activate your chakras and discover what you have stored there. You will feel nervous, agitated, afraid or uncomfortable in some way if you are not grounded while you activate your spiritual system.

Grounding connects your first chakra to the planet. The first chakra is located near the base of the spine. It is the only chakra located differently in female and male bodies. The other chakras are located in the same positions. The difference is because of the difference in location of the gonads. In men the first chakra is located lower in the body near the testicles. In women the first chakra is located higher in the body between the ovaries.

As you learn to ground, be aware of the location of your first chakra according to the gender of your body.

Your relationship to this reality is affected by the gender of your body and the way you ground it. Grounding can help you accept your body as it is and learn to use it to your best advantage.

Sit in an upright position, hands and feet separated and feet flat on the floor. Have your spine straight and take a few deep breaths. Close your eyes and turn within.

Be aware of your first chakra near the base of your spine. Create an energy connection from your first chakra and allow it to flow through the material world to the center of the Earth.

Take a few deep breaths to help the flow of energy from your first chakra to the center of the Earth. The flow of energy is your grounding cord. Your grounding cord connects you to the Earth.

You can be grounded at all times. You can be grounded when you are sitting, standing, walking, or in any position. You can be grounded when in a car or any conveyance. Your grounding can attach you to the planet at any time or place. This grounding cord is your spiritual connection with the planet and your body. By creating your grounding at all times, you stay connected to this reality.

Your grounding cord creates a safety line for you, an energy connection to this Earth. Grounding helps your body feel safe and balanced. It keeps you in touch with what you are creating in your physical reality. Grounding is the safest way to make your body real to you as spirit.

You can also use your grounding cord to release energy. Simply let energy flow down your grounding cord to the center of the Earth. You can release excess energy when you feel tense. You can let go of foreign energy to make space for your energy. You can release any type of energy down your grounding cord. Releasing energy is important in your healing process as it cleanses and creates space for growth.

Another way to let go of energy is to bend forward and dangle your arms toward the floor. This releases energy from your arms, shoulders and head. After this release you can sit up and resume your daily activities or continue your meditation.

Bend forward and release energy now. Sit up again and continue your exercise.

Create your grounding cord from your first chakra to the center of the Earth. Breathe deeply and allow your grounding cord to carry away any tension in your body. Be aware of how your body reacts to being grounded and releasing the energy.

Remain grounded and stand and walk around the room. Experience your grounding as you do this. Return to your seat and increase the flow of energy down your grounding cord to increase your grounding. Again release any tension from your body down your grounding cord.

The technique of grounding is used throughout the exercises. While it is presented briefly here, it is recommended that you practice grounding frequently. You can be grounded while standing in lines, working, practicing a sport, or doing anything in your life.

Ground from your first chakra to the center of the Earth. Be still and listen to your heartbeat and your breathing. Pay attention to how your body feels.

In this quiet space with your eyes closed say the Lord's Prayer silently to yourself. Notice your experience. Repeat the prayer as often as you like.

Use your grounding cord to release any lies about this powerful prayer. Let go of any experience of having to say this prayer as a punishment.

Be grounded and say the Lord's Prayer again and enjoy the healing.

Bend forward toward the floor and release energy. Sit up and continue your activities.

Whenever you meditate, begin by grounding. Your grounding cord will help you to be in charge of your creativity. It will give you an effective, efficient way to release energy and will put you in charge and in control.

The following techniques and the chakra exercises all depend on your use of grounding. Without grounding you are not able to focus enough to fully experience the other exercises. Ground and enjoy the journey within.

CENTER OF YOUR HEAD

When opening the chakras it is beneficial to be in the center of your head. This is the location of the sixth chakra which contains your information on clairvoyance or clear seeing. The center of your head is the space where you as spirit are meant to reside while in your body. It is the place where light is reflected through the pineal gland into the body.

The center of your head is where you see clearly as spirit. By viewing life from the center of your head you allow a neutral view. You are neither positive nor negative but balanced. You can see the full picture and make your decisions from a spiritual perspective. You can be neutral and not judgemental when you are centered here.

If you judge yourself or your creations, you will block your spiritual growth. Being neutral is essential so you do not sabotage yourself through judgement, muddled views or emotional reactions. The ways of spirit and of God are not the ways of man. The clearest spiritual view we have in the body is from the center of the head where we have clairvoyance and neutrality. From this space we can see our way along the spiritual path.

Sit in a straight-backed chair, feet flat on the floor, hands separate in your lap and your spine as straight as possible. Take a few deep breaths.

Create your grounding cord from your first chakra to the center of the Earth. Release any tension in your body down your grounding cord.

Focus your attention into the center of your head. This space is above and behind your eyes. You can draw imaginary lines through your head: one from your forehead and another one from your temple near your ear. Where these lines would intersect is approximately the center of your head. Be there and experience this space.

Notice how you feel being in the center of your head. How does your body feel having you there? Allow time for your body to adjust to you, the spirit.

Take a few deep breaths and relax your body. Send any tension down your grounding cord. Be in the center of your head and allow you and your body to adjust to you being there.

You are spirit and you have immense energy. Your body has much less energy. When you move into your head you affect your body. You may even frighten your body. It is necessary to take time to allow your body vibration to increase to accommodate you, the energetic being. Your meditations will bring this about. As you use the techniques you will cleanse your system and raise the vibration of your body.

Again focus into the center of your head. Move above your head to experience the difference. Move back into the center of your head.

Use your grounding cord to release any energy or tension resulting from being in the center of your head.

Be grounded and in the center of your head and be still for a few moments. Allow you and your body to adjust to you being present.

Bend forward and release energy to end your meditation. Sit up and continue your reading.

It takes time and practice to use the techniques effectively. Practice being in the center of your head any time. You will discover it is a great asset to be neutral in your daily life. Be in the center of your head often during your meditations so you can be in touch with the reactions of your body to your spiritual work and can respond to it.

As you work with your chakra system, be in the center of your head so you can move smoothly through your growth. When you are centered in neutral you can see the temptations and overcome them. You can see the detours and avoid or shorten them. You can be neutral about your creations and begin to see life as a spiritual journey.

THE ROSE SYMBOL AND SPIRITUAL CREATION

The symbol of a rose has been used throughout history to represent the opening of the soul to God. It is the Western symbol, just as the lotus is the Eastern symbol. A soul unfolds to God as a rose opens to the sun. This symbol is used because it is neutral and represents simplicity and beauty. The rose emerges from the soil of the Earth to become a thing of great beauty.

Spirit is here on Earth to grow and mature. We must create to learn. In this Earthly plan, spirit is a co-creator with God. By creating, spirit learns and grows and discovers what does and does not work. It is necessary for us to use our God-given ability to create in order to learn.

We use the symbol of the rose to practice our spiritual creativity. The technique of creating and exploding a rose is used to fine tune our creativity as spirit. We can use the rose symbol to help us release unwanted energies and concepts and cleanse our system. By creating and exploding a rose, we can clear whatever we need to from our system.

The rose symbol can also be used to cleanse the chakras. This helps us take greater control of the system so our growth is easier. We can clear foreign energies or non-beneficial energies with the rose symbol and open the way for our own clear flow of energy and information. By creating and exploding a rose we enhance our energy flow and clarity.

Create your grounding cord from your first chakra to the center of the Earth. Focus your attention into the center of your head.

Visualize the image of a rose about six inches in front of your forehead. Take a moment and admire your creation.

Explode the rose. Let it disappear. Create a new rose and admire that creation. Explode it. If you have difficulty seeing a rose, know that it is there and you will eventually cleanse your system enough to see the rose.

Create and explode roses at your rate for a few moments to practice this technique.

Think of one thing in your life you do not like. Be aware of what is keeping you from changing this thing. Create a rose and put the block to changing into the rose. Explode the rose and the block. Create and explode roses for this block several times.

Release energy down your grounding cord. Notice how you feel after exploding the block to your growth. Be aware of your body's reaction.

Ground, be in the center of your head and create a rose in front of you. Explode the rose. Create and explode roses until you feel comfortable with this technique.

The rose can be used to practice spiritual creativity and to cleanse the system. Use the symbol during your meditations to help you focus your attention and to heal yourself. By simply creating and exploding the rose you use your creativity, cleanse your system, and activate your chakras. You can also focus on a particular creation as you use the rose. The more you use this symbol, the more you own its meaning for you and the more you allow yourself to open spiritually.

RUNNING ENERGY: EARTH AND COSMIC

Everything is energy. Energy is always in motion. Different things have various levels of energetic motion. A rock has a very slow vibration of energy, while the movement of energy in a flower is faster. The human body has a higher level of energy. Spirit has a much higher vibration than anything physical.

We run our energies automatically. This technique is to help you run your energies consciously, in a particular pattern. This pattern helps you to be in touch with the Earth and your body, and with yourself as spirit and the Cosmos. Being aware of both aspects of yourself helps you function and create as you wish in this reality.

Using earth and cosmic energies also helps you to deal with your chakras and balance your system. This balance allows you to heal yourself. Balance lets you create safely and consciously. Balance helps you be in control of and use your chakras more fully.

Earth energy includes the vibrations of this planet. Cosmic energy consists of the vibrations of the Cosmos. Both energies can be seen clairvoyantly as colors. There are no limits to the variety or amount of energy available, so there is an infinite amount of energy for us to use. We will use a gold vibration of cosmic energy since this is a neutral, healing energy. This vibration also raises the vibration of the body so we can use it and create through it more as spirit. We use the vibration of earth energy that is comfortable to the body. That varies from person to person.

Assume your meditation posture and relax by breathing deeply.

Create your grounding cord from your first chakra to the center of the Earth. Focus into the center of your head. Create and explode several roses.

Be aware of the chakras in the arches of your feet. Bring earth energy up through these chakras to channels in your legs. Let the energy run through the leg channels to your first chakra near the base of your spine and then let it flow down your grounding cord.

Be in the center of your head and grounded. Create and explode roses to cleanse any block to your earth energy flow.

Allow the earth energy itself to melt away any blocks in the feet chakras or the leg channels. Let the energy blocks melt and flow away down your grounding cord.

Be still and enjoy the flow of your earth energy and allow your body to adjust to you consciously manipulating this energy.

Some people are naturally grounded and tuned in to earth energy. Others will need time to adjust as they have not had their attention on this aspect of their reality. Allow time to practice running your earth energy to become comfortable with it.

Re-establish your grounding cord. Be in the center of your head. Create and explode a few roses. Run your earth energy up your leg channels to your first chakra and down your grounding cord.

Draw a vibration of clear gold energy down to the top of your head. Let the gold energy flow from the top of your head down channels along each side of your spine to your first chakra. Let the gold energy flow gently and smoothly.

At your first chakra, mix the earth and cosmic energies and let them run up channels along each side of the chakras through the body. Run mostly cosmic energy after the third chakra at the solar plexus.

Let the energy flow out the top of your head like a fountain and flow all around your body. Also let some energy flow from the cleft of your throat down channels in your shoulders and in your arms and out the chakras in the palms of your hands.

The lower chakras relate more to earthly aspects of your creativity and the upper chakras relate more to spiritual aspects. Therefore, you need to run mostly cosmic energy in the upper channels and chakras. Diminish the amount of earth energy after the third chakra and run mostly cosmic energy from the fourth chakra up. Running these energies cleanses your system just as flowing water cleanses.

Run your earth and cosmic energies. Make sure you are grounded and in the center of your head as you run these energies. Create and explode roses to enhance the energy flow.

Be still and enjoy this flow of energy. Let the earth and cosmic energies cleanse any blocks in the channels as warm water would melt ice. Do this for some time to become accustomed to running energy.

Bend forward and release energy to end your meditation. Sit up and resume your activities.

Running energy activates your chakras. Consciously running your energies helps you take control of your system and heal yourself. Running earth and cosmic energies is a technique to cleanse the chakras. Practice running your energies until you are comfortable with this technique.

Put all of the techniques together for your meditations. Running your energies for thirty minutes to an hour a day helps you clear your energy system. This cleansing is necessary to allow for the opening and full use of your chakras. Practice and perseverance are needed to learn the techniques as well as to continue to use them.

As with all things, these techniques must be used in order to be effective. You cannot read this and think about it and have it affect you. You have to practice the techniques and use them on a regular basis. It is like physical exercise. You cannot benefit from an exercise program by reading about it. It is necessary for you to get up and do it for it to work for you.

Meditation is the most valuable thing you do every day as this is your time for communication with yourself and your God. Allow yourself this conscious cleansing time to create a clear communication. Meditation is essential to all of your spiritual work.

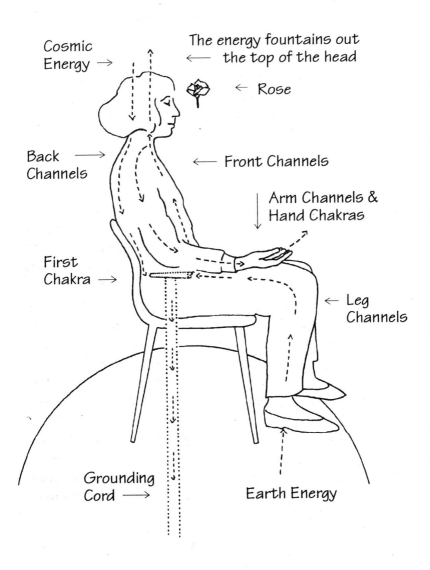

Figure 1. Running Earth and Cosmic Energies, and Groundin

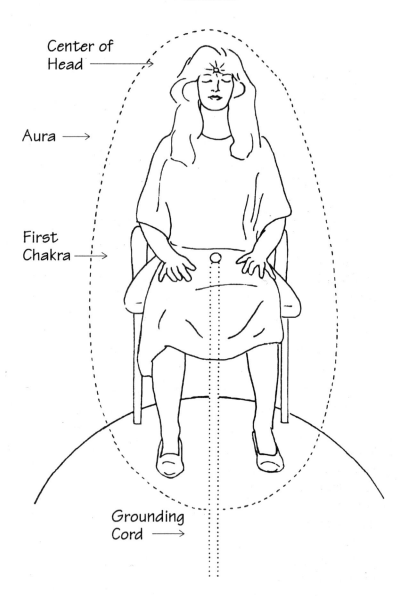

Center of
Head

Aura

First
Chakra

Grounding
Cord

Figure 2. Aura, Center of Head and Grounding Cord.

THE AURA

The aura is an emanation of the energy of your chakras. The layers of the aura relate to the chakras: the first chakra projects the first layer of the aura, the second chakra the second layer and so forth. We will relate to the seven major layers and the seven major chakras.

The aura changes in vibration as the chakras change in vibration. There is no set or ideal vibration or color for any of the chakras or aura layers. We are always changing and growing. If we establish a set vibration and do not allow for variation, we do not grow. The main consideration is keeping the aura and the chakras clear and bright and in motion. If they are cloudy or the energy is dense or not moving, they are disturbed, invaded or somehow not functioning correctly.

By using the meditation techniques you raise your vibration. Over time, the vibrations of your chakras and your aura come to an appropriate level for you as spirit to operate through effectively. Even then the vibrations will vary according to what you are doing or experiencing. If you try to match another person's vibration, or an idea of the perfect vibration, it will keep you from growing and healing yourself. Everyone is unique and has unique lessons. The chakras are information centers and we each have different information. If we all had the same vibration in each chakra, we would think, look and act alike because we would have the same information through which to create.

The aura is a changing, flowing energy halo. Being conscious of your aura helps you see how you are manifesting energy. It allows you to see if the energy is yours or another person's, in the present or past, clear or cloudy. Your aura is your window to the world. Your aura indicates how you are relating to the world. Through this energy window you see the world and the world sees you. Owning your aura is important as it is a major statement of yourself as spirit.

Ground from your first chakra to the center of the Earth. Be in the center of your head. Create and explode roses. Run your earth energy and gold cosmic energy.

From the center of your head be aware of your aura. Ideally, it is all around you. If it is not, bring it all around your body. Allow it to flow under your feet, above your head and equally in front and in back of and around your body.

Be grounded and centered and allow your aura to flow around you like the halo from a candle.

From the center of your head, expand your aura so it fills the room. Notice how this feels. Retract your aura so it is two inches around your body. How does this feel?

Relax your aura so it is between six and eight inches around your body. Be aware of how this feels.

You can expand and contract your aura as needed. You may want to draw it in close to you when you are in a room full of other people so you do not have to experience their reality. You may want to expand it when you are walking in the woods to experience your surroundings. Ideally your aura is filled with only your energy, so keeping it six to twelve inches around you will help you maintain your personal vibration.

Ground, be in the center of your head, and be aware of your aura around your body. Create and explode roses to help your aura relax and flow smoothly. Take time to do this as it cleanses your aura.

Increase your grounding, focus in the center of your head and run your earth and cosmic energies. As your energies flow out the top of your head and through your aura, let them cleanse your aura. Experience the healing flow and allow time to adjust to it and enjoy it.

When you are through with your meditation, bend forward and release energy. Sit up to end your meditation.

As you cleanse and own your aura, you create consciously. You become aware of how you are creating on the seven levels of the chakras. For example, if your second layer is a dark red, you see that your body is angry and you can communicate with the body to find a solution to the problem. Knowing that the second chakra relates to emotions and a darkness to any color indicates disturbance, you soon learn how to interpret the information in your aura.

The aura is much easier to see and interpret than the chakras. It is simpler to learn to read and safer to relate to since the chakras are intricate and contain so much information. The more you practice working with your aura, the more proficient you become with interpreting it. Your aura shows outwardly the state of your chakras. Your aura displays what you are creating in your energy system. Learn to know your aura and you will know yourself.

PRESENT TIME

Present time refers to the ability to focus as spirit in the present moment. Spiritually viewed, time is an illusion. We have time in the physical reality to allow for growth and change. This gift of time allows us to experiment with our creations and to rectify mistakes. Time is one of the energies we as spirit learn to manipulate when we manifest in physical bodies.

As spirit in a body, we have the ability to put our attention in the past, the present and the future. Even with this gift of time, it is beneficial to have our attention in this life and in this moment. The point of power is in the present. Healing takes place in the present. As we get acquainted with the chakras, we discover the need to bring them into the present and to relate to them in present time. The body is always in present time. God is always in present time. We have to learn to refocus in the present to heal ourselves and communicate with our body and with God.

Most people have learned to put their attention into the past or the future to avoid what they are creating in the present. We learn to do this in childhood and continue it through life. If things are painful, frightening, or causing unhappiness, the soul projects its attention into the future or the past to escape the difficult present. Everyone has had the experience of fantasizing or day-dreaming. This is a way to project into the future. Reminiscing about the past can be an escape from the present. Either direction takes one away from the power of the present moment. In the present you can best heal things from the past and plan for the future.

When you focus into the present, you face the reality which you have created. In the present you can respond to a situation and change it if necessary. If you are not paying attention, you may create problems you will need to face in the future. When you are not focused in the present, you may create ideals you cannot meet. While as spirit you can project your attention through the energy of time into past or future, it is most healing to deal with the chakras in the present.

Focusing into the present takes practice as we have all gotten in the habit of escaping into the illusion of future or past. This present time focus can be learned in meditation and in daily life. You can teach yourself to focus in the present simply by paying attention to what you are doing. While you prepare a meal, take a bath, walk, or talk with friends, or meditate, pay attention to the moment. When you find your attention wandering, bring it back to the moment. You will learn about yourself and your world. When you are in the present you will eventually feel the presence of God.

Create your grounding cord from your first chakra to the center of the Earth. Focus yourself into the center of your head.

Run your earth energy through your feet chakras and leg channels and down your grounding cord. Run gold cosmic energy down the back channels to the first chakra and up through the system in the front of the body and out the top of your head. Let the energy flow down your arms and out your hands.

Create and explode roses for a moment to adjust your system. Be aware of your aura and bring it all around your body. Be still and experience this flow of energies.

From the center of your head, be aware of your grounding cord. Get the concept of bringing your grounding into present time. Be still and let it happen.

Be aware of your earth energy and bring it into present time. Let the flow of earth energy bring the feet chakras and leg channels into present time. Be aware of your gold cosmic energy and bring it into present time. Allow the gold energy to bring the back, front and arm channels into present time.

Create and explode roses to clear anything interfering with your present time focus. Take time to focus on cleansing any block to being in present time by creating and exploding roses for the block.

Be in the center of your head and be in present time. Listen to your body: your heartbeat and your breathing. Let your body rhythms draw you into present time. Tell your body that you love it. Be quiet and in present time.

Bend forward and release energy. Sit up and end your meditation.

Present time is so simple it will easily elude you. You will need to focus on it. By practicing your meditation techniques and bringing your attention into present time during your daily life, you will learn to have this focus. Present time will bring you back to life as your life is happening in the present.

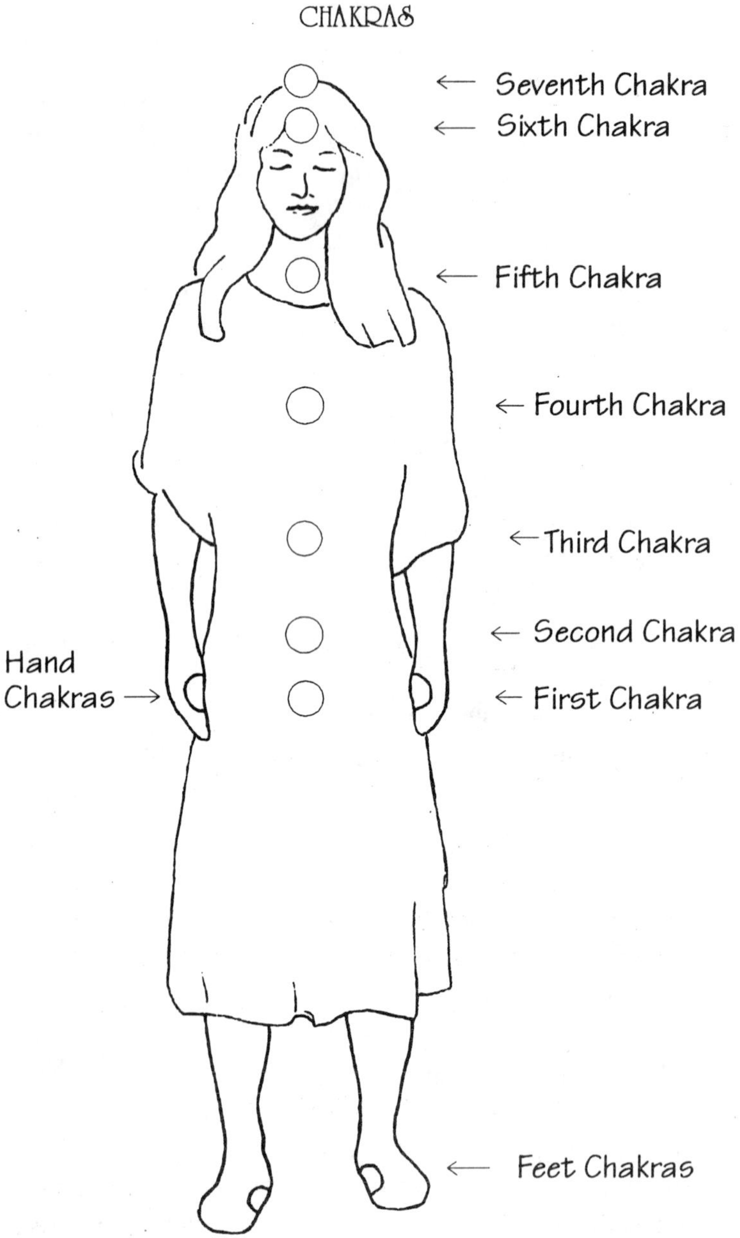

CHAKRAS

← Seventh Chakra
← Sixth Chakra

← Fifth Chakra

← Fourth Chakra

← Third Chakra

← Second Chakra

← First Chakra

Hand
Chakras →

← Feet Chakras

Figure 3. The Major Chakras.

THE CHAKRAS

All of us have an energy system which enables us to manifest as spirit in the physical realm. One part of this system is the chakra system which contains our spiritual information and energy. The chakras are located in the body along the spine and go all the way through the body. Simply described, the aspect of the chakras we will deal with is shaped somewhat like a cone with the larger end at the front of the body and the smaller end at the spine. The chakra spins like a wheel in two directions, both clockwise and counterclockwise. Energy flows through the energy centers from front to back. The chakras are in a state of health when they are moving and energy is flowing through them. If the energy slows or the chakra stops turning, the chakra does not function properly. Other aspects of the chakras are located outside of the physical body. While we will not relate to this aspect of the chakras, these areas are cleansed as we work with the chakras inside the body.

We have an unfathomable amount of information in each chakra. We will speak of them here in simple terms since we cannot begin to relate to their complexity. This approach provides information and techniques to help us discover in our own way and time the wealth we have stored in our chakras. The information we have in each chakra is there for us to use, to learn and to grow. We create opportunities to test the concepts we have stored

47

in the chakras, to clear unwanted concepts and to create new concepts. The information in the chakras is not static but constantly changing. As we mature, we discard old ideas and develop new ones. This growth is reflected in the chakra system.

The word chakra is a Sanskrit word meaning "wheel" which clearly describes these energy centers. The chakras, when viewed from the front, appear as bright colored wheels or circles turning. The Eastern view of the chakras as flowers opening is descriptive and simple. This perspective is beautiful and helps avoid the Western desire to intellectualize. We will not describe every physical detail of the chakras in order to avoid intellectualizing them. Our focus is on the importance of learning to work with them. To function fully in the physical reality as a spiritual being, it is necessary to use the information and energy in the chakras.

When you run your earth and cosmic energies, the energy flows from the front to the back of each of the chakras as it flows up through the system. Chakras are similar to the lens of a camera or the iris of the eye in that they can open and close as needed. Grounding, centering, running energy, creating and exploding roses, and being in present time are techniques to help you get in touch with and use the information and energy in these centers. The techniques also help you adjust the chakras to the appropriate openness.

The term "opening" means to unseal and access the information in the chakra. It does not suggest that any chakras need to be completely open, or that more open is "better." It is not beneficial to have any chakra totally open or completely closed. Work with the chakras needs to be done gently and carefully so that no damage is caused. The goal is control, since with control the chakra can be used and accessed at any time. Once you learn control, you can make adjustments when needed. Having a chakra too open or too closed can be harmful to the energy system. You need to observe caution as you first activate the system. Adjust your chakras gently and slowly. When working with power, use patience and caution.

The opening of the chakras, or information centers of the soul, is definitely a challenging game. We need to be careful not to get too serious about this learning experience and at the same time do it with respect for ourselves and others and with reverence for the spiritual information.

We learn more rapidly and easily when we are amused. Our amusement is meant to help us take the lessons lightly, not irreverently. If we are serious and heavy, or false in our amusement, our growth process slows and may even stop since we are no longer enjoying our spiritual journey. The discovery of the chakra system and its information is ideally a joyous process and we often need to remind ourselves of this along the way. The energy level of God is best described in this reality as enthusiasm. When we are enthusiastic, we are attuned to God and our lessons in this world are light and easy.

There is no correct order in which to activate the chakra system. Each soul is unique and therefore will approach this reality in its own way. We all have much to contribute and can do it only through our personal process. Some people tune in to lessons in one or two chakras per lifetime. This allows for intense concentration. Many people open each chakra a little at a time, allowing the entire system to be in balance. Others begin with one chakra and travel methodically through the system. There are as many ways to focus on the system as there are souls.

We begin with the first or root chakra because it contains information on how to relate to the physical reality. We also connect ourselves to this world from the first chakra. Beginning our lessons with the first chakra grounds or connects us to this reality where we must develop our comprehension. As we learn about the first chakra, we learn to understand ourselves as spirit and how we operate through a body. We eventually learn to bring our spiritual energy all the way into the body to the first chakra.

The next chakra we focus on is the sixth which contains our information on how to see clearly as spirit. We need to see clearly in order to see what we are doing and operate safely as we unseal the other chakras. We encounter many temptations and obstacles as we do this work so we need to see what is truth for us. If we depend on other people's concepts, we do not operate from our own. We need to see what is our truth and what is a lie for us by using our sixth chakra. We learn to identify our own vibration so we can clear anything foreign. Clairvoyance provides us with the neutrality to see what to change, what to be patient with and what to leave as is.

By developing the abilities in the sixth chakra early in your spiritual development, you discover the difference between what is yours and what is not. For example, you want to keep the information about using the toilet, but you may not want to keep the emotions you adopted from your mother about it. While the toilet training is necessary to be accepted in most societies, your mother's emotions about it are not. This simple example can help you see the need for your clairvoyance. Cleansing the chakras requires clarity so you do not remove needed information as you clear the information that is not beneficial. As you work with your chakras, remember your amusement and the distinctions will be easier to make.

In this lesson you will then proceed from the second to the third and fourth chakras and then to the fifth and seventh chakras. Once you have learned something about each chakra and learned how to use the basic spiritual techniques, you may work with your chakras in a variety of ways. In your meditations you will be cleansing the chakras from first to seventh. As you run your earth and cosmic energies it flows through the chakras from first to seventh. You can choose to put your attention on any one chakra depending on your needs and personal growth.

Meditations are included with each chakra description. Allow yourself to sit quietly and meditate on what you read and on each chakra. There is also a guided chakra meditation to use in cleansing and owning all of the chakras. It is important to be clear on what is your truth and how you can use the information in your own life. You can do this by sitting quietly and using the meditation techniques. As you center in your neutral space and ground to this reality, you allow a safe communication between you and your body and between you and your God. You create a conscious space to see your own truth and your way within to God.

THE MAJOR CHAKRAS

CHAKRA	LOCATION	INFORMATION
First chakra	Near the base of the spine	How to relate to this reality
Second chakra	Just below the navel	Emotional and sexual
Third chakra	Solar plexus	Energy distribution
Fourth chakra	Sternum or Heart	Affinity
Fifth chakra	Cleft of the Throat	Communication
Sixth chakra	Brow	Clairvoyance
Seventh chakra	Crown of Head	Knowing
Hand chakras	Palms of hands	Creativity and healing
Feet chakras	Arches of feet	Earth energy

Figure 4. Table: Description of the Chakras.

THE FIRST CHAKRA

The first chakra has your information on how to relate to this physical world. You ground from the first chakra. Your earth and cosmic energies meet and flow through the first chakra. You bring your spiritual energy into the first chakra to spiritualize your body. The first chakra has information about how to deal with your male and female energies. The first chakra is extremely important.

Taking charge of the first chakra is essential in our spiritual development. If we do not become senior as spirit to the way we relate to the physical reality, the body will relate to it in a continually more bestial manner. We are here on Earth to learn to take charge of our bodies, not to have them take charge of us. Many beings have allowed their bodies to gain an inordinate amount of control over them and have a great deal of work to do to reverse this trend.

The first chakra is the only one located differently in male and female bodies, as the gonads are in different places in these two bodies. In the female body the first chakra is located between the ovaries. In the male body it is located above the testicles. By accepting this difference, you allow for the differences in the male and female body vibrations. The female body has a higher vibration than the male body and needs the extra grounding provided by the slightly higher location of the first chakra. The gender of the body we have chosen is important for our learning process. The first chakra contains a great deal of information about our bodies and how to relate to them.

Often people spend less time on this important chakra than is necessary. If you put attention on your first chakra and your grounding, you create a firm foundation for the rest of your work. If you do not own your first chakra, you will find yourself without an anchor, blown by the winds of change. You will experience a great deal of change that you will cause by focusing on yourself as spirit. Prepare for your growth by creating the necessary foundation of owning your first chakra and grounding.

Part of relating to this physical world is learning how to survive: how to provide food, clothing, housing, and other body needs. Since there are so many different cultures and customs, it is clear that there is no "correct" way to relate to the world. We also can see that each individual has his or her own ideas about how to approach survival issues. Therefore, it is important for each of us to turn within to find our own answers about survival and all other aspects of relating to this world. When we turn within, we find the spiritual information we need. We find God within and our lives gain a new light that brings ease and joy to all aspects of life, even our physical survival.

Our relationship with this reality can be one of enthusiasm, creativity and power. When we reawaken spirit in our lives, we bring the joy back. We can be like "the lilies of the field" and find our "burdens light and easy." The first chakra has our spiritual information that we can use to make this joyous relationship possible. Clearing old patterns and lies from the first chakra allows the spiritual information to shine through. We can then create a harmonious relationship between spirit and body and make our lives what we want.

There are other aspects of relating to this reality which we often forget in our focus on the survival issues of the body. Information about our healing energy is found in the first chakra. We also have the ability to adjust the first chakra to keep the body from being afraid when there is no present reason for fear. This can help us heal many situations. The healing ability we have as spirit to clear pain and other debilitating energies from our system has been largely forgotten. Our healing energies have been focused on the physical and we have neglected the spiritual realm much too often. Everyone has a wealth of healing information in the first chakra. The information we have there is what is correct for each individual.

Keeping a spiritual perspective about relating to physical reality is important when dealing with the first chakra. We create many tests and lessons for ourselves to learn and grow. Childhood accidents abound as children practice operating in a physical body using both their own concepts and the ones of the protective adults around them. We are taught the physical limits but not the spiritual perspective, and we bring this blindness into adulthood.

As we gain control of the first chakra, we realize that everything is energy and we can manipulate energy. We become aware that the physical world is energy and we only need to remember our spiritual information to know how to relate to the world harmoniously. Our only real limits are our doubts and our fears. The doubt and fear cause us to limit ourselves to the physical perspective of the intellect, and our intellect cannot comprehend the magnitude of spiritual creativity.

The fear of death is the greatest limit to our mastery of our relationship with this Earth. We have gotten so lost in the belief that we are just our bodies that we have forgotten we are spirit. The body wants to be in control and not allow us our spiritual awareness because it does not want to be aware of its mortality. We are immortal. The body is like a shell or husk or vessel which we will shed when we finish with it. The more power we have given to the body, the more afraid we are of death since it is the body that fears death. When we allow ourselves to be senior as spirit, we begin to relate to the body with love and teach it to accept its death. As we accept our immortality, we can train the body to accept its mortality.

When we begin to open the first chakra, we see the survival issues we have created. We see our concepts and expectations of our world, other people's concepts, and how we relate to this reality. We do not need to be caught struggling with survival issues. We only create survival situations to learn something and grow through it. We can create whatever we need to learn a given lesson. Many happy lives have been lived in what most would consider poverty. We have also experienced misery in the midst of physical abundance. Every life can be lived with joy or unhappiness. When we view the first chakra lessons from our spiritual perch in the center of the head, it becomes possible to overcome the difficulties we have created. We can create whatever we need physically and spiritually and can find joy in our creativity. By using the first chakra correctly, we allow our spiritual and physical realities to be in harmony. Spirit and body are meant to work together. This information is in the first chakra even if it is dormant. The key is to create and maintain a spiritual perspective of our physical interactions.

As a child you learn what does and does not work according to other people's responses. You learn how to operate in this reality from others' beliefs. Often your own beliefs are buried under the barrage of external information. This is a major reason you need to meditate on and own your relationship to this reality and your first chakra. You may come into the body with a clear and joyous relationship to the world and learn from others that you need to adopt a serious, unhappy relationship with it to fit into the society you have chosen. You may have entered the body to bring joy to the entire group and allowed yourself to be overwhelmed by their beliefs. The adoption of others' beliefs can cause a great deal of unhappiness and confusion if you do not remove the foreign concepts from your system.

You may have been taught that you must struggle, work hard and compete to survive in this world. If you have a life lesson of being gentle, quiet and introspective, you will be fighting your own nature with the concepts you have been taught. Unless you release the foreign ideas, you could do many inappropriate things in your life. A friend of mine became a doctor although he was better suited to be an English professor. He died of stomach cancer after years of not being able to digest all the pain and anguish he saw in his work. His nature was too gentle for the demands of the work he was programmed to do.

The first step when opening and owning a chakra is cleansing it of foreign energies. All of us learn from those around us when we enter the Earth plane. We take in the beliefs of our parents, siblings, teachers, peers and so forth about how to keep our bodies alive and well, how to make a living, how to relate to one another, and many other things. Unfortunately, some of this information does not work for us since each soul has unique creations to experience. We can be especially confused by information gathered from someone in a body of a different gender. We also need to keep in mind that some information gathered from others is valid for us. This all highlights the necessity for developing the spiritual techniques of grounding and being in the center of the head early in our spiritual development.

Use the techniques to get acquainted with your first chakra and to discover the information you have stored there. Work gently and slowly and you will not create problems. You have an entire lifetime to discover what you have in your chakras. Relax and enjoy the process.

Ground from your first chakra to the center of the Earth. Be in the center of your head. Run your earth energy up through the feet chakras and the leg channels to your first chakra and down the grounding cord. Experience the flow of earth energy through your first chakra.

Bring in gold cosmic energy through the top of your head and along the channels on each side of your spine to the first chakra. Mix the earth and cosmic energies and bring the energies up through the channels in the body along each side of the chakras.

Allow the energy to fountain out the top of your head and flow all around you. Let some of the energy flow from the cleft of your throat, down your arms and out your hands.

Be aware of your aura all around you. Make sure it is under your feet, above your head and in front and in back of your body.

Create and explode roses to adjust your energy flow and your aura. Take a few moments to relax with your energy.

From the center of your head be aware of your first chakra near the base of your spine. Be aware of the earth and cosmic energies flowing through it from front to back.

Allow the flow of energies to wash away any foreign energies from your first chakra. Let these energies cleanse and clear your first chakra.

Be aware of your grounding cord flowing from your first chakra to the center of the Earth. Let any foreign energy flow from your first chakra down your grounding cord. Simply release the energy and let it go.

Be in the center of your head and create and explode roses for any foreign energy in your first chakra. Allow the energy to flow out of you into the rose and explode the rose.

The techniques can help you cleanse the chakra so you can get to your own information. This cleansing process will take time as you have been collecting foreign energy all of your life. Allow time every day to do this cleansing and healing exercise and you will soon know your own way to relate to this reality.

Ground, be in the center of your head and run your energies. Bring your first chakra into present time. Allow any past or future time energy to flow down your grounding cord.

Be aware of relating to your physical reality from the present. Let go of any past life ways of relating to the world that are no longer appropriate.

Create and explode roses for any energy in your first chakra that is not in the present.

You open and learn about your first chakra as you cleanse it, bring it into the present and discover what information you have stored there. When the chakra is cleansed and in present time you can use the information with greater ease.

Be grounded and centered and be still. Be aware of how you now relate to your world. Release anything you do not like down your grounding cord.

Own the ways you relate to this reality that you do like.

Allow your first chakra to fill with gold energy and let the gold neutral energy heal it. Release the gold energy down your grounding and let the first chakra be at its most healing present time vibration.

Use this exercise regularly in your daily meditations and you will learn about your first chakra and your unique way of relating to this reality as spirit. Run your energy to activate and cleanse your chakras. Use your grounding and establish a firm foundation for your spiritual creativity.

THE SIXTH CHAKRA

The sixth chakra, located at the forehead, has information about clairvoyance or clear seeing. This is the ability to see auras, chakras, pictures, beings without bodies and other spiritual phenomena. As we open and develop this ability, we learn what is true for us and begin to separate truth from lie in our personal space. Clairvoyance helps us see how someone else's beliefs color our reality. Developing our clairvoyance helps us to develop neutrality which is essential in opening the chakras. We need to be able to forgive ourselves and others and we cannot do that without neutrality.

Owning our clairvoyance, or the ability to use our spiritual eyes, is one of our most important developmental steps. We need this chakra's information to avoid the pitfalls of judgement and other limits of a strictly physical perspective. How many have lost faith in God by trying to explain a trauma in physical terms only. Without the spiritual perspective provided by the view from the sixth chakra, one can easily get lost in lies and judgements and despair.

We need a clear view for healing. It is necessary to see what is before we can decide what to change. We need to maintain an unemotional perspective to help with any change. For example, when a loved one is in a state of distress, if we can see from neutral, we can help him. When we become distressed along with him, we lose our healing power and our ability to help him through his lesson. Many people identify neutrality with being cold and unfeeling. That is entirely incorrect. Neutrality gives us a spiritual perspective from which to operate above the emotional pull. Neutrality provides us with the clarity and power necessary for healing action.

One pitfall when opening the sixth chakra is believing you see everything and therefore know what is best for everyone. This is an ego problem that can block further development. This temptation will cause a clairvoyant to give people advice instead of seeing and saying what is. The ego is a temptation on every level of development, so if it is faced early, it is easier to overcome. Learning to see yourself as you are is essential in seeing others. If you discover your ego is tied up in your spiritual development, then you need to take the time to face that and clear your ego involvement. The information in the sixth chakra helps you do this as you learn how to be neutral and forgiving with yourself.

An ego problem that occurs for some people in the process of opening spiritually is believing that you are a disciple, Jesus the Christ, Mary the Mother or some other famous figure in the Jesus Christ story. This phenomenon can occur as you are developing the aspect of yourself that the disciple, Jesus or Mary represent in the Christ story. Each character in this spiritual play shows us a step in spiritual development. Each demonstrates a different lesson and vibration. We have to go through each step to reach the Christ level of awareness. If you have the experience of one of these souls, this is a time to rejoice as you are opening and developing. Do not be afraid that you are crazy. Do not believe that you are a reincarnation of these teachers either. You are a developing soul going through the stage of spiritual development this soul exemplifies.

Since the Jesus story is the story of the development of the individual soul, each figure in the story represents a specific growth process. The events in the life of Jesus, including the Christmas story, the Easter story and all of the experiences of Jesus, are also steps in the development of the soul. As you open yourself spiritually, you learn to recognize the lesson taught by each of these spiritual role models and by each of these events. You can eventually learn how to interpret and use the meaning of the characters and events in your own development.

Every soul is able to be a Christ. Christ means anointed or appointed one. Christ is one who is enlightened. The significance of Christ is the experience of God in man. Every soul on Earth is meant to achieve the Christ experience. Our ultimate purpose for being on Earth is to manifest the Christ.

The wonderful souls, such as Jesus, Mary, Moses, Buddha, Lao Tsu, Mohammed and many others, that showed us how to do this are always ready to assist us. We need to use our clairvoyance to see that we are unique and have our own way of manifesting the Christ within. Allow yourself to follow the Christ path without trying to be someone else. Your lesson includes learning to be yourself. Being enlightened is being yourself. The trick is learning who you are and how to manifest your unique personal vibration.

We need to be vigilant, even in the development of this most helpful of abilities, so we do not put physical rules on our clairvoyant ability. We must remember that we see the world through our own eyes whether they are the physical or the spiritual ones. Our own views of life color our reality and this affects our interpretation of everything we see. We need to see what is and not what we want to see. As we develop, the ability to be in touch with ourselves and God enables us to maintain our spiritual perspective and not get lost in the physical world.

While opening the sixth chakra it is wise to remember that you can only give to others what you can have for yourself. So if you are not neutral or clairvoyant about yourself, how can you pretend to provide this for others? You can read other people's "pictures" and life creations, but are you able to do this from neutral, without judgement or punishment? Opening any of the chakras is primarily for your own spiritual development. If you are called to assist others, you will know you are ready to do so by maintaining your communication with God.

The development of the sixth chakra is most helpful with the opening of the remainder of the system. As you begin to unseal the other chakras, you may find that the power of the information you have stored in them will challenge your ability to stay in your sixth chakra in neutral. It is always a balancing act to allow the emotions without being swept away by them. You have to learn to allow the body to be as it is and not be overcome by it. You will not reach a perfected state where you will no longer have to learn about yourself. The fact that you exist in a body gives you constant challenge. Even after you have opened and cleared the chakras for years you will find issues you have to face in yourself. Living a spiritual life is an active experience.

We are spirit and we need to practice our spiritual abilities and use them in our daily life as well as in meditation. If we continue to use this spiritual focus daily, clairvoyance assists us to become more neutral with our life lessons. When we focus our attention in the sixth chakra, we focus ourselves as spirit on light, neutrality and the spiritual perspective.

By looking from the sixth chakra, we can see when we are acting on our own and when we are being manipulated by others. We see why we chose our parents, mates and children as partners in learning. We gain clarity and in doing so gain our own power because we know what is and cease to be fooled by the illusion of the physical veil. From the sixth chakra we gain a full view that explains to us the purpose of our life and shows us the most beneficial path to our goals.

Our life path will sometimes take us away from those we love. These separations occur if we no longer need those interactions for our learning process or if we each have different paths to follow. The spiritual perspective of clairvoyance helps us be neutral about the times we must be apart as well as the times we are together. We can see that as spirit we are one. We separate into bodies to learn and help each other learn. When we are through with a lesson, the "teacher" is no longer needed and both parties can move on to the next lesson.

Whether the lesson is difficult or easy, when we see it from the sixth chakra, it has greater meaning and the other participants have understandable roles.

The opening of the sixth chakra lets us see our path and ourselves as spirit moving along that path. We can see when we take a misstep or a detour and more easily move back onto our own path. Clairvoyance lets us see ourselves and others as spirit. It is part of our healing system. It shines light on all things in our life and helps us find our way back to God. Open the sixth chakra with joy. It enables you to see and it can set you free.

Create your grounding cord from your first chakra to the center of the Earth. Focus your attention into the center of your head.

Be aware of the sixth chakra located in your brow, extending from the front to the back of your head. Increase your grounding.

Bring the earth energy up through your feet chakras and leg channels to the first chakra and down your grounding. Bring the cosmic energy down through the channels in the back of your head, along the spine, to your first chakra. Mix the earth and cosmic energies at the first chakra and move them up the channels on each side of the chakras running through the body.

Let the energy fountain out the top of your head and flow around you through your aura. Let some energy flow down your arms and out your hands.

Be in the center of your head and grounded. Be aware of the gold energy flowing through your sixth chakra from the front to the back. Enjoy this healing flow of energy.

Let any excess energy flow out and be grounded off. Let the flow of neutral gold energy cleanse and clear your sixth chakra. Experience this cleansing for some time.

Create a rose in front of your sixth chakra. Explode the rose. Be aware of you using your sixth chakra as you do this.

Create and explode roses to release any block to using your sixth chakra. Continue to allow your energy to run.

Create and explode roses to release any foreign energy in your sixth chakra. Use the flow of gold energy to cleanse any foreign energy from your sixth.

Be in the center of your head and bring your sixth chakra into present time. Allow any energy from the past or future to flow out of the chakra with the flow of energy.

Be grounded and centered and continue to allow the gold neutral energy to flow through your sixth chakra.

After spending time cleansing and owning your sixth chakra, you can more easily use it to see clearly. By viewing the world from the neutrality of the sixth chakra, you gain control of your creativity. You also have a neutral place from which to work as you unseal the other chakras.

Be grounded, centered and run your energies. Make sure your aura is all around you.

Create and explode roses to enhance your flow of energy. Create and explode roses to exercise your sixth chakra.

Be aware of one thing you are not neutral about. Create and explode roses to clear any foreign energy from this issue.

Use your grounding to release any blocks to seeing this creation from neutral.

Bring the issue into present time. From the center of your head allow yourself to see the lesson you are trying to learn from this experience.

Ground, create and explode roses and run your energies to clear interference to learning the lesson. View the creation from neutral and notice how you relate to it as spirit.

This exercise can be used for any life experience. Allow as much time as you need to deal with an issue. You will find some are easy and become clear instantly, while other creations have more energy in them and take time to work through. Allow your use of the techniques to assist you to learn to operate from the sixth chakra and the spiritual perspective.

By using the sixth chakra you will develop the ability to read yourself and make changes from a conscious, aware state. This helps you avoid detours and mistakes on your life journey. For example, you may be angry with a friend and carry this disturbance on for years if you operate from an emotional level. If you practice the techniques and use your sixth chakra to see the situation from neutral, you will see the spiritual lesson and learn it more quickly. You can forgive your friend and yourself and continue with a happier life.

The sixth chakra is essential in the unsealing of the other chakras. It gives you the neutral, spiritual view you need to avoid problems and temptations and to see things as they are. From neutral you can see that you are a capable, immortal, powerful being and you can see that everyone else is, also. As you open the other chakras, you can avoid being overwhelmed by the body's responses, such as strong emotions. You can see the fear or doubt as it emerges and clear it before it deflects you from your path.

The sixth chakra is the reflector of light in the body. We are here to reflect light and need this light to see who we are and where we are going. Turn on the sixth chakra and you turn on your light so you can see through any darkness. Use this light to see the information you have stored in your other chakras and open them to light.

THE SECOND CHAKRA

The second chakra is located just below the navel. This chakra relates to clairsentience or clear feeling. The second chakra contains the information about one's own emotions and sexuality. It is through this chakra that we feel the emotions and sexuality of other people. We often associate it with feeling other peoples' emotions more than our own because we use clairsentience early in life as a communication and survival technique. "How does mother feel?" "Do I get food when she is angry?" While feeling others' emotions is part of one's clairsentience, it is not the core. Experiencing ourselves in this reality is more important for learning our lessons than experiencing others and their emotions. We need to experience our own emotions to know what is occurring in our body. Since the body is the experiential system for us as spirit in the physical reality, we need to know what is going on within and around it to operate as we wish.

We are trained to be tuned in to other people's emotions. "Be nice." "Do not hurt others' feelings." It is necessary to train ourselves to be in touch with our own emotions. This can be a frightening experience if our own emotions feel unfamiliar or overwhelming. We may feel quite uncomfortable with our own emotional messages at first, and we may judge them instead of responding to them. We may believe that our anger is "bad." This will block us from realizing that the body is sending us a message that it is unhappy with a situation or frightened and dealing with the situation aggressively.

Whatever emotional message the body is sending, it is up to us as spirit to deal with it since it is the body's response to something we have created. Each emotional message is different. Some emotions we may need to overcome during a lifetime and some we may need to nourish. The key is to be aware that the emotions of the body are the body's way of communicating to the spiritual being. It is vital to unseal and learn to use the second chakra because we need to learn to communicate with our body in order to use it effectively.

Our emotions are part of our communication system with our body and from our body to other bodies. By accepting our emotions as the communications that they are, we eliminate judgement of our emotions. Then we can feel the emotions and respond as we need to in any situation. If we feel the emotion of fear and allow it to freeze us, it will block normal functioning. When we listen to the body we can discover what causes the fear. When we face the source of the fear and move through it, the fear no longer paralyzes us. By listening to the body's emotional message we solve our physical problems.

It is necessary to learn to control the second chakra and the emotions. This does not mean to deny the emotions. Denial will only block communication.

Without communication between the soul and the body a great deal of confusion occurs. Feeling and accepting the emotion allows one to respond to the present reality instead of pretending it is nonexistent. Everyone knows what it is like to deny reality as it is. It is like living with an elephant and pretending it is not there. You get stepped on and pushed around a lot. Acceptance allows one to respond, while denial causes one to malfunction in some way.

Emotions are the voice of the body. We are not seeking to eliminate emotions; we are trying to learn how to use them and be in control of them. The emotions are part of our learning process in the body. We need to learn how to interpret and use them. When we know what our body is saying, we can be responsible for our creativity through the body.

As spirit we have to learn how the body works. Just as we need to know how to operate our car to drive it, we also need to understand our body to use it properly. The emotions help us do this by letting us know what is happening at any given time with the body. If the messages are garbled by foreign energy or lies about what is a good or bad emotion, then we will not get clear information. We will not be able to operate effectively in our bodies, just as we will not get a functioning car if we try to run it without oil or with foreign matter in the gasoline. Keeping the second chakra clear is essential to clear communication with the body and clear creativity in life.

We can eventually learn to take control of the emotions to the point of manipulating the body as we wish. This requires discipline and concentration. We must strongly desire this and work on it continuously to achieve it. Most people will find learning to understand their own emotions and learning to respond appropriately to them adequate for one lifetime.

Be aware that anything emotional is from the body and not a spiritual message. When you realize this, you have learned an important lesson in spirit-body communication. You need to be aware of this when opening the second chakra since the emotions have great power and will pull you into the body's world. You are not the body. You are spirit. Opening the second chakra is one of the greatest challenges in maintaining your spiritual awareness because the second chakra is the body's main communication channel to you and the body has a lot to say and wants to be in charge. It will try to pull you from your position of control in the sixth chakra into the body's world of the second chakra. The body is like a child in its desire to have your attention in order to have control of the situation.

One of the most powerful pulls of the body is the sexual energy located in the second chakra. Sexual energy is physically and spiritually for creative and communication purposes. Physically, it is for the creation of bodies. As male and female come together physically, another body is created. Spiritually, sexual energy allows for the higher vibration of the spirit to enter the Earth plane and establish the unique vibration of the entering being. Sexual energy is a high vibration. A high vibration is needed for the spiritual entry into this physical reality.

The vibration of spirit is much higher than that of body so an increase in vibration is necessary when we have a transition between the two realities. The transition times are the times of highest vibration. The high vibration of sexuality is needed at conception, when a being is entering this physical reality. Other examples of increased vibratory flow are at birth, at the instant of death, and when a "channel" brings another being into her body.

Because the sexual energy is a high and intense energy, it is a temptation to put one's entire attention on this one aspect of reality. Many souls become so caught in this one physical aspect that they take lifetimes to free themselves from its pull. Often they spend several lives on the opposite end of the dichotomy where they condemn sexuality as they attempt to find their space from it. They may eventually balance their relationship with sexuality and use it beneficially. Sexuality is one of God's creations and can be a thing of beauty. It only becomes ugly when we misuse it or abuse it. When used as an enhancement of communication and creation in the spiritual sense, it can change one's perspective and bring great joy. We can eventually learn how to use the high vibration of sexuality within our own space to raise our vibration for meditation and communication with God.

The physical aspect of our sexuality has a great deal of power because it is associated with the survival of the species. It is especially strong in females since sexuality is tied to the creative process of pregnancy and childbirth. Female bodies of all species have a powerful drive to create and sexuality is part of that drive. The complexity of sexual behavior in males and females is all based on the desire to create. Societies have devised amazing rituals built around this drive. Individuals also create their own sexual behavior patterns to attract a mate. The hormones in both male and female help to stimulate sexual desire to attract a mate and create a new body. The physical system associated with procreation is complex. It takes dedication to learn to be in charge of it.

This physical pull from our sexuality is one of the most powerful of our seeming "beasts." It helps to have our amusement when learning to take control of our sexuality. When we believe we cannot live without something such as sex, we need to step back and regain our spiritual perspective. It can help to get our perspective by watching other species act out their sexual drive. Fluffing of feathers, calls in the wilderness, and various other performances have both beautiful and comic aspects. Watching birds sing and strut or horses neigh and fight can remind us of ourselves and remind us we are in bodies also.

When we see the difference between the body and ourselves as spirit, we learn what is the body's desire and what is our own. The body may have a desire to have sex with ten different people, while the being may want to have sex with one particular being to create the correct vibration for the conception of a body for a third being. Or the being and body both may want to create a conception. Programming can block this action and cause the being to sublimate the desire by doing something else. There are so many possibilities in this physical world it is essential to keep a spiritual perspective. When you navigate as spirit you stay on course and avoid dangerous waters.

Learning to understand how your body works and how you want to use it allows you to deal with your sexuality from a spiritual perspective. You learn that you do not have to act out the sexual desires of the body and that you can be in charge as spirit with your sexuality. You can eventually learn to use the high vibration of your sexuality for your spiritual purposes within your own space. It is important to see and know what you as spirit want when dealing with the power of sexuality.

When we get back our neutrality, we realize that our sexuality simply provides another learning opportunity: a vibration we can learn to use as spirit. If we judge sexuality as either the best or the worst, as good or bad, we will not gain the balance we seek in relation to this high body vibration. We created sexuality for a purpose and it is up to each of us to learn its purpose in any individual situation or lifetime. We may experience everything from total celibacy in a lifetime as a monk to total degradation in a lifetime as a slave. We may even be working on a similar lesson in as seemingly different realities as these. We may experience the joy of using our sexuality to create a body for another soul. Some may even learn to use their sexuality to increase their spiritual vibration in the body. All physical energies can be transformed into spiritual vibrations for spiritual purposes. Each soul is unique and has its own lessons and its own relationship with its body and its sexuality.

It is not necessary to practice celibacy to become spiritually enlightened. Most people will not gain the seniority over the body to become celibate. Very few souls achieve this level of seniority. Many people become physically and spiritually ill trying or pretending to be celibate. Anyone can learn to become senior enough to their body to see how they want to relate to their sexuality and use it for their learning process. As one opens and grows spiritually, all aspects of the body lose power. As spirit gains power in the body, the physical pulls, such as sexuality, decrease naturally. This happens gradually over time.

Most people feel a great increase in their sexuality when they first turn on their spiritual awareness so there is a time of intense challenge between the spirit and body. When you awaken the system, everything turns on, including the sexuality. It is necessary to decide how you want to relate to your sexuality so it does not take over your life.

Whether we are dealing with our emotions or our sexuality it is important to clear foreign energies from the second chakra. It is also essential to bring it into present time. We must clear past painful experiences so we do not create our present emotional and sexual life through pain or someone else's decisions. We need to own this chakra so we do not get manipulated by it.

The second chakra, in both its emotional and sexual aspects, contains a wealth of information for us to use in this reality to create what we need. We only need to learn to listen to and hear the messages of the body and then translate these messages into our spiritual perspective so we can use the information constructively in our work here on Earth. By gaining control of the will of our body we gain control of our creativity on Earth.

Create your grounding cord from your first chakra to the center of the Earth. Focus your attention into the center of your head. Your neutral perspective allows you to deal with your emotional information in a healing manner.

Be aware of your second chakra located just below your navel, running through your body from front to spine. Increase your grounding and be aware of the energy in your second chakra.

Bring the earth energy up through your feet chakras and leg channels to your first chakra and let it flow down your grounding cord.

Let the cosmic energy flow down to the top of your head and through the channels in the back of your head, along your spine to your first chakra. Mix the earth and cosmic energies there and let them flow up through the channels in your body.

Allow the energies to fountain out the top of your head and flow all around your body. Let some of the energy flow from the cleft of your throat, down your arms and out your hands.

Be in the center of your head and grounded. Be aware of your second chakra. Experience the energy in your second chakra.

Each chakra has a different vibration. Feel the vibration you are using in your second chakra. Feel the vitality of energy you have here.

Let the energy flow through the chakra from front to back as it flows through the channels. Meditate on the flow of energy for a few moments. Notice if there is any change in the energy after you run energy through the chakra.

From the center of your head, be aware of the main emotion from your second chakra. Release any judgement about that emotion down your grounding cord.

Talk with your body about its emotion and what your body is telling you with this emotion. Learn to understand what you are experiencing in your body. Create and explode roses for any interference to experiencing your emotions.

Be in the center of your head and be grounded. Be aware of your second chakra and own it for yourself. Create and explode roses to remove others' emotions from your second chakra.

Be still and meditate on your emotions and their information for you as you create through your body. Focus on one emotion at a time.

Be in your sixth chakra to avoid being overwhelmed by your emotions. Create and explode roses to clear your system and increase your neutrality about your emotions.

Be grounded and tune in to your sexuality in your second chakra. Experience your sexuality. Create and explode roses to release any judgement about your sexuality.

Release other people's energy about your sexuality down your grounding cord. Own your relationship to your sexuality.

Be aware of how you as spirit want to relate to your sexuality. Create and explode roses to release foreign energy. Release judgement down your grounding cord.

From the center of your head put your attention on your second chakra. Create and explode roses to clear any foreign energy from this chakra. Use your grounding cord to release energy from it.

From neutral, bring your second chakra into present time and release energy from the past or future.

Own your second chakra so you can have a clear communication between your body and you. Use the meditation techniques to help you own it and clear foreign and inappropriate concepts and energies from it. Your second chakra is a significant aspect of the will of your body and you need to learn to be in charge of the body's will to be in charge of your creativity through it.

THE THIRD CHAKRA

The third chakra has information about how we distribute our energy in this reality. It distributes vital energies throughout the body and energy system and is located at the solar plexus. Information on our experiences out of the physical body and our memory of these experiences are also located in the third chakra. Our distribution of energy determines a great deal about how we create our reality. If we distribute energy to our healing channels, we have less focus on other aspects of our reality. If we focus more on our spiritual awareness, we have less energy for our body reality. There is no good or bad connected with this distribution. We need to distribute our energies according to what we need to learn in order to accomplish our present life goals.

How we distribute our energy determines what we are creating. We may need to focus on healing ourselves for some time and will turn our energy inward. This can take many forms, from meditating a great deal, to going hiking, to being sick in bed. We may need to focus on a creation that involves others, such as a relationship, and use our energy for healing it. We need to keep our spiritual view to allow our energies to flow where they are needed. Any change in our energy distribution can cause a healing because it readjusts our system. By simply putting our attention or energy on something, we can create a healing. As we distribute our energies throughout our day, we focus both on self and others, internally and externally, spiritually and physically. When we maintain our spiritual perspective the energy flows without effort.

Notice how in one day you change the distribution of your energy from one chakra to another. In any given day you most likely change the flow of energy several times, depending on what you are doing. Conscious use of the third chakra gives a greater control over your system as you knowingly shift your energy flow. You can tune your energy up or down depending on the need of the moment. A great deal of energy is needed during an emergency and not much energy at all during a day of rest. When you take control of your third chakra, you can have the energy when you want it and rest your system when you wish.

A challenge in controlling the third chakra is the temptation to use the power found there for physical purposes only. We discover the unlimited source of energy and then try to create our own reality without consideration for the Divine plan. We may be like a child with his first bicycle, wanting to ride wherever and whenever we wish without consideration for anything else except our own desires. Beneficial use of energy demands spiritual awareness to gain a broader perspective of reality.

A different problem can arise when we are afraid of our power. If we do not own the ability to manipulate our own energy, then someone else will use our energy for their purposes. We may find ourselves doing something we do not approve of and being manipulated by our own energy if we do not own it. This lack of ownership can come from many things. It often arises from a lack of self-worth we may develop by holding on to others' criticism. We may also fear that we could misuse our energy and therefore do not want to be responsible for it. If we are afraid of using our energy, we are better off if we do not open the chakra system. We are responsible for our reality so we must own our creations. We need strength to allow ourselves the power of consciously distributing our energy and that strength comes from our relationship with God. As we open the third chakra, our spiritual perspective is essential so we do not get lost in the power games of trying to control others. Our energy is meant to be used to create within our own universe.

The experiences we as spirit have outside our physical bodies and the memory of those experiences are another aspect of the third chakra. We are spirit and we have a physical body and an astral body in this earthly reality. We also have bodies of different vibrations that we use in other realities. The astral body is emphasized here as it is the other body we use to create in the Earth plane. We use it to experiment with possible scenarios before we manifest them in the physical body. We also use it to experience aspects of ourselves we cannot experience in the physical world. The astral body is less dense, lighter, a higher vibration, and is not bound by the rules of the physical body. The astral body is what people are seeing when they say they have seen a "ghost."

In the astral body we can experiment with a possible future or heal aspects of our past. We can create scenes with other beings that we may later create in the physical body. We can heal many things and create our life on Earth by experimenting in the astral body before we manifest them in the physical body. We are not as bound by physical limits in the astral body. We need to learn to use the astral body and the third chakra which contains our information about it in order to control our creativity.

As spirit we can also have out-of-body experiences which are completely out of any of our bodies. We are spirit; we are not any of our bodies. Bodies are our vessels in which we create and communicate to enhance our growth. Some of these out-of-body experiences we consciously remember and many of them we store in the third chakra for spiritual reference. Much of this information is not comprehensible to the physical body but is necessary for us as spirit. The emphasis here is on the astral body experiences as these are our most conscious out-of-body experiences and relate to our life on Earth.

Our memory of experiences outside the physical realm plays an important part in validating ourselves as spirit. In some lifetimes we are so veiled from the spiritual realm that we can be aware of our spiritual selves only through the memory of our out-of-body experiences. We can also have a life of being aware both physically and spiritually where we are conscious whether in or out of a body. We may have the thrill of seeing our own body while we are outside of it or remember an experience we had in our astral body and then created in our physical body. The memory aspect of the third chakra is important because it validates us as spirit and lets us know what we are creating on a larger scale. It gives us a broader view of our spiritual creativity.

One thing that confuses many people is thinking that astral body experiences are dreams. Often, astral body experiences and the memory of them are described as dreams. Dreams occur when the body sorts through experiences or memories and when there is an overload of information or disturbing experience. An astral body experience is when the spirit is in the astral body. Dreams and astral body experiences are easily told apart since dreams are confused and disjointed, while astral body experiences are just like physical body experiences in their reality factor. We see things much as we would in the physical body. But on the astral we have abilities we usually do not allow ourselves to have in the physical body, such as the ability to fly or walk on water. We are also able to deal more freely with interactions and emotions in the astral body than in the physical body since there are no ethics on the astral plane.

Because the astral body has a lighter, higher vibration, we are able to manipulate it more easily than the physical body and accomplish things we are not developed enough to do in the physical body. The memory of these astral experiences is important to our spiritual development. Our astral experiences are as much a part of our creative experience in this world as the experiences in the physical body. The memory of the astral experiences is located in the third chakra so we need to own this chakra to know what we are creating as spirit. What we create on the astral plane we will manifest on the physical plane unless we consciously make a change.

A stumbling block to the opening of this information is confusion between this physical reality and the astral reality. When we confuse them, we may find ourselves having difficulty making sense out of our lives and trying to make things happen now that are plans for the future. While it is helpful to be aware of non-physical realities, we must also remember the importance of maintaining our ability to function in physical reality. We have come here to learn a lesson and if we allow astral body experiences to become our main focus, we may not accomplish our life mission. It is tempting to spend a great deal of time in the astral reality because it has no ethics and requires no effort in its creative process. We may feel closer to spiritual reality and long for that greater sense of union so we may be tempted to spend more time out of the physical body than is appropriate for our lessons here. The key is to learn a balance between these two realities and listen to our inner voice and guidance from God.

We can use our astral experiences to learn about ourselves and our relationships with others and to clarify our goals. We may be having trouble with our mate and find the solution to our problem when we leave the denser vibration of the body. The body might house some programming from our mother that is not appropriate for our marital relationship. We might keep wrestling with the foreign concepts until we leave the body and the programming in it. We can use our astral body to get in touch with our own information. We can then bring our information and solution into our physical body and use it to clear the foreign programming which does not work. That way we change our relationship with this reality. The key is to use our astral body experience to enhance our experience in this reality, not to escape this reality.

As we open the chakras, we learn about ourselves, what we like and what we dislike. We learn our strengths and our weaknesses. We are tempted to hide our weaknesses instead of clearing them, and we must remember that we uncover them to turn them into strengths. Any time we are tempted to be overly delighted with our strengths or too serious about our weaknesses, we can always get back on track by finding some amusement with ourselves. It is helpful to remember that we are an important part of a powerful and dynamic whole.

Ground, center and run your earth and cosmic energies. (See pages 34-36 for review.)

From the center of your head be aware of your third chakra located at your solar plexus. Be aware of the chakra going from the front of your body to your spine.

Increase your grounding. Let gold energy flow through your third chakra from the front to the back. Enjoy the flow of energy.

Allow any excess energy to flow off the back of the chakra and go down your grounding. Be still and allow this cleansing for a few moments.

Create a rose six inches in front of your forehead. Explode the rose. Create and explode roses to release

89

any block to using your third chakra. Allow your earth and cosmic energies to continue to run.

From the center of your head be aware of any belief you have that blocks your personal power. Let your flow of earth and cosmic energies wash away the belief. Create and explode roses to release the belief. Release energy down your grounding cord.

Take several deep breaths and relax your third chakra. Let it relax and release the belief that blocks your power.

Breathing deeply helps you relax your chakras, especially your third chakra. If your abdomen feels tight breathe deeply and let it relax. This will help you open your third chakra and allow it to turn freely. Since your distribution of energies is here, you need to keep the energy in your third chakra moving freely so you can have the energy necessary to function as you wish.

Ground, center and run your earth and cosmic energies. Bring your awareness into present time.

Bring your third chakra into present time. Allow the gold cosmic energy to flow through it and cleanse foreign energy from your third chakra.

Use your grounding to release any blockage to your out-of-body experience and memory. Let the gold energy cleanse blocks to your memory and experience.

Allow time to own your out-of-body memory and experience. Use grounding, centering and running energies to help you own this spiritual ability. Create and explode roses to release blocks to owning your experience and memory.

Use your flow of energies and grounding to cleanse limits to your distribution of energies. Select one limit at a time and take time to cleanse it from your third chakra and other parts of your system.

Your distribution of energy, your out-of-body experience and out-of-body memory are important ingredients to spiritual mastery. You need energy and knowledge to have power. You need power to create in any reality. The information in your third chakra gives you the power you need to be spiritually aware, to heal and to create your life mission. Use the techniques to help you access the information and energy you have in your third chakra.

THE FOURTH CHAKRA

The fourth chakra has the information about being in a state of oneness. We can experience oneness with all things. The most important aspect of the fourth chakra is the ability to experience oneness with God. The fourth chakra is located at the chest or sternum and is often called the heart chakra. It contains information about affinity. Affinity is a force that combines things or energy and creates the experience of oneness. It can be observed and experienced in all aspects of life from chemical reactions to spiritual attractions. Often this force of affinity is based on affection. When spirit is in control of the chakra, affinity is neutral. Spiritually perceived, affinity is neither positive or negative but neutral. It brings energy together into a state of oneness.

When we get the fourth chakra confused with other information centers, we complicate our reality with lies. We often bury this beautiful information under a barrage of body phenomena. We confuse body issues with our relationship with God. We confuse spiritual oneness with physical togetherness and think that merging with others on a body or personality level is the same as spiritual oneness and affinity. Merging and oneness are not the same. Merging causes us to experience the physical reality of another, such as their emotions. Oneness allows us to experience another as spirit. We need to learn to have our oneness without getting lost in it; we need to learn to relate to it as a spiritual experience, not a physical one. While in a body, we need to retain our sense of self to better relate to the physical world in our daily living. In meditation and prayer we can experience oneness with God when we let go of self. When we gain spiritual perspective and control we can experience our unique self and our oneness with all things.

When we get confused between affinity and merging we attempt to take responsibility for others. When we merge with them, we then try to change them into our image of them, instead of accepting them as they are. When we are merged we want to take control of the other person's life. Since we are merged, we believe their life is ours and we need to be responsible for them and control them. This lie about merging versus affinity also convinces people that good deeds are the avenue to oneness. Good works are a way of expressing our desire to give and have no relationship to oneness or affinity. We can do a good deed just for the joy of doing it without any consideration for the outcome or recipient.

When we do not operate the fourth chakra correctly, we get caught in ethics and lose sight of the existence of the vibration of affinity. When we use the fourth chakra correctly, we can tune in to this oneness any time. We only need to be aware of our affinity to use it and enhance our reality with it. Everyone longs for the sense of oneness that comes from opening this chakra. We can have it when we clear the lies and the confusion from our system. We only need to be still and tune in to ourselves as spirit to experience our oneness with all things. Doing physical things does not bring us closer to our affinity and oneness. Opening this aspect of ourselves and allowing our affinity and experience of oneness is a spiritual experience.

A stumbling block in opening the fourth chakra is wanting to run away from the other energy we often hide or store here. This is usually the favorite storage center for pain. We seek oneness and affinity with others and when we do not experience it in our relationships, we pull in the other person's pain to communicate. We try to alleviate our loneliness by filling the space with both the other person's pain and our own. In this way we develop a reservoir of pain and loneliness in the place where we have our information about affinity and oneness. We even store emotional responses such as hate, fear, guilt or even sexuality in the fourth chakra when we do not experience the affinity we are seeking. Often we do this because we do not develop or allow our patience and neutrality. These would help us see that others are immersed in their physical world too much to experience oneness and affinity. Many people have closed their fourth chakra as a survival technique, but this creates the opposite of the desired effect. We do not have to do this to survive our experiences. If we allow the affinity and oneness in the fourth chakra, it makes it possible for us not only to survive, but to live and create in this world with joy.

When we open our affinity and find pain, we look outside ourselves for the creator of such madness and fight the realization that we created it ourselves. Then the opening of one of the most joyous centers can create trauma in our reality. We start blaming others for the things in our lives we do not like. We look for the ones who did not love us enough. We enhance the sense of isolation we developed and make ourselves more miserable, until finally we clear the pain and loneliness and allow the affinity vibration to prevail. The energy blocking our affinity is what we have put in our own way. We have to face this and clear what we do not like. Owning the creations we do not like is a major step in everyone's spiritual development.

When functioning correctly, the fourth chakra is a source of great joy. The sense of oneness brings new awareness and communication. By experiencing oneness with others, you can more easily accept them as they are. By allowing your oneness with God, you can learn to love yourself. This oneness helps you realize that you are part of a whole. When you experience this oneness, you seek your part in the total pattern. There is satisfaction and peace in fulfilling your unique part.

The opening of the fourth chakra also brings us a new awareness of the things in this world which we do not like and we have to adjust to that part of reality as well. We become as aware of the ugly as we do of the beautiful, and we must guard against judging the overall plan. From our limited view of the world the temptation is to try to make the world all beautiful, loving and perfect. We can lose track of the fact that God's view takes in the entire spectrum and that the meaning behind many things is hidden from us in our limited view. We can easily be tempted to play God from the fourth chakra. We feel all that is and then want to fix everything according to what we believe is "right."

It is a challenge to experience the affinity and oneness without needing to "do" anything. It is only necessary to experience it and be aware that our manifestation of affinity is affecting the reality of all others. We do not need to do physical things to share this affinity. We automatically share it by developing it and having it within ourselves. By experiencing the oneness and affinity within self, we do not need to leave the body to have a sense of God. We can even share this affinity with our body. All of our spiritual abilities must be developed within, and only then can we share them with others. One must have affinity for oneself before experiencing it for anyone else.

Many people get out of balance with the fourth chakra and the other chakras. It is especially important to balance the fourth and the sixth chakras. The fourth chakra contains affinity, an aspect of love, and the sixth chakra contains light, an aspect of truth. We need both to be whole and to function fully. When we balance the fourth and the sixth chakras, we have affinity and light. If we have only one, we are out of balance and cannot create with our full spiritual power.

Development of the fourth chakra helps us to learn love. The fourth chakra contains affinity and oneness which are aspects of love. Love also includes communication, neutrality, knowing and reality. Love involves all of the chakras. Do not try to make your fourth chakra your only source of information for love, or you will not understand this vibration. By only comprehending part of love, you will misunderstand and misuse it, and this will bring you frustration and confusion. Let the fourth chakra be what it is and let go of trying to make it everything.

Our action-oriented reality often interferes with the opening of the fourth chakra because it does not allow for the creation of quiet time. A quiet internal focus is central to our communication with the Cosmic Awareness and essential for the opening of the fourth chakra. The oneness of affinity is ultimately oneness with God. We need to be quiet to experience God.

Ground from your first chakra to the center of the Earth. Focus into the center of your head.

Run your earth energy up through your feet chakras and leg channels and down your grounding. Run your cosmic energy down through the top of your head and along the spine to the first chakra. Let the energy run up through your body and out the top of your head. Let some of the energy flow down your arms and out your hands.

Bring gold cosmic energy through the cosmic energy channels. Let it flow through the fourth chakra from front to back cleansing the chakra.

From the center of your head be aware of your fourth chakra. Create and explode roses for any foreign energy in your fourth chakra. Let go of other people's energy in your fourth chakra as you cleanse it.

You experience your affinity and oneness with others more fully when you have space between you. Just as plants grow better when they have space to grow, so do we as spirit. Allow your experience of oneness without merging; they are not the same. When you clear other people's energy from your fourth chakra, you can experience your affinity for them without experiencing their energy. You can have your own affinity. They can have their affinity.

Ground, center and be sure your energies are flowing. If there is a block to the flow of your energy, create and explode roses to clear the block and use your grounding to release it.

Bring your fourth chakra into present time. Create and explode roses for energy in your fourth chakra that is not in the present.

Be aware of someone for whom you have affinity. Use your flow of energy and your grounding to let go of any limits to your affinity.

Be aware of someone you do not like. Release the blocks to having affinity for this person by creating and exploding roses, grounding and running energy to clear the barriers. Experience your affinity for this person. Allow time for this and repeat the exercise as often as necessary.

Be grounded, centered, and be still. Be aware of your fourth chakra and its message of affinity and oneness. Listen.

Be still and experience your affinity for yourself.

Be in the center of your head and grounded and experience your oneness with God.

Bend forward and release energy. Sit up and return your attention to the physical world.

Do not think that the fourth chakra is sweetness and niceness as we humans define "nice." It is not. The fourth chakra has great power. When you learn to control and use the fourth chakra, you have control of your creativity and power. This comes from experiencing your oneness with God and knowing that all of your creative power flows from God. Opening your awareness of your fourth chakra allows you to experience God.

Learn to control the fourth chakra, and you will open to the world of affinity and oneness. You can experience your oneness with all things. You can have your communication with God. This is not an easy lesson. Many people open the fourth chakra last because it has great power. God is power. God is love and light. God is life.

THE FIFTH CHAKRA

The fifth chakra is our communication center. There are five aspects of communication concentrated here: broad and narrow band telepathy, clairaudience, pragmatic intuition and the inner voice. Telepathy is communication without words to one person, to a small group or to a large group of people. Clairaudience is communication with beings without bodies and over long distances. Pragmatic intuition is knowing practical information such as who is calling on the telephone. The inner voice is communication with yourself. With all of these spiritual interactions we send and receive pictures, symbols, formulas, vibrations and other spiritual signals. These communications allow us to know what is occurring for us as spirit.

The lowest form of communication is words. Words help us make ourselves real to our bodies and real in the physical world. When we verbalize our awareness, we not only make it more real for our own body, we also share the information with others. Verbal communication allows us the opportunity to project our energies into the physical world. We have a great impact with the spoken and written word. These are our beliefs made manifest in this world. Our thoughts and beliefs are energy forms through which we create, so verbal communication is a way we create spiritually.

In opening and using the fifth chakra consciously, we need to realize that thoughts, pictures and other spiritual communications are as powerful as actions and that our words are powerful also. We often attempt to negate the power of words in order to excuse our misuse of them. We use words as weapons and then attempt to justify the damage they cause. We also go to the opposite extreme and let our ethical systems limit our full use of words and dictate what we can and cannot say or write. Often we need to project a strong message to be heard or understood, but we do not allow ourselves to do this because we believe it would be impolite. We remain unheard or misunderstood because of our own limits. We also express ourselves in spiritual ways that get the message across without our taking responsibility for the message. We may say one thing and think another. We may say how much we like someone and send the telepathic message that we hate them. The hate is what they will receive no matter how strong our lie and facade. We have to realize that we communicate spiritually whether we acknowledge it or not.

Telepathy is the ability to communicate without words spoken. We can communicate with one or two people or a large group. We also receive telepathic communication from others. If we are not controlling this ability, we can experience a great deal of confusion because we will be hearing messages that do not relate to us. We may be allowing too much information to come into our communication channels. We become overloaded with information and it is as if we were listening to the radio, TV, stereo, and someone talking all at the same time. Eventually, none of it makes sense. When we pay attention to our spiritual communication and take control of it, we can allow only what pertains to us at a given time so the communication can be used in this reality. The key is to focus and control the communication, not to test how much you can have.

Clairaudience is the ability to communicate with beings without bodies and over long distances. This ability is important to own since it will be used by others if we open this chakra and do not take control of it. We can experience a clairaudient conversation with a being without a body at any time or place. We often communicate with our spirit guides who do not have bodies, and when we do, we are using our clairaudience. Most people have experienced this but have turned off this ability because of their fear. It is no more or less powerful than communicating telepathically with a being in a body. Our clairaudience also gives us the spiritual freedom to communicate without the limits of time and space. We can be in touch with a friend across the globe and enjoy the experience of our spiritual communication and connectedness.

We need to be in charge of our clairaudient ability so that we do not pick up information which does not concern us. We can tune in to so much that our challenge is in focusing, not in hearing everything. We accomplish a great deal when we focus this ability because we begin to send and receive what is significant to us. When we are unfocused, we get so much interference we do not find this communication level useful. Many people have the experience of hearing voices that are not physically present. If this is a beneficial interaction for you, it is possible for you to have it and be in charge of it by owning your clairaudience. If the voices are disturbing or destructive, you can tune them out by turning your clairaudience to a different frequency or by turning it down. You do not have to listen to any message. You can say no and turn the message off, just as you would turn off your radio if you do not like a program.

Since communication is such an important focus and delight for us as spirit, the communication chakra is especially joyous to open and master. We begin to realize that we are not alone and that we can be in touch with any one at any time and place. We let go of the physical limits and begin to enjoy a new level of spiritual awareness as the communication flow increases. The trick is learning what to listen to as we open. The easiest solution is to use our inner voice for confirmation and clarity.

It is necessary to establish communication with your body and with God to maintain a safe and comfortable growth process. The inner voice is an important focus in the fifth chakra because it allows you to be in touch with yourself as spirit and with God within. As you learn to depend on your inner voice for validation and confirmation, you build your confidence in your spiritual information. The inner voice is the most important aspect of the fifth chakra for personal growth.

Your inner voice allows you to hear your own information. The inner voice sounds just like you. It is located in the fifth chakra at the cleft of the throat.

When you learn to talk with yourself, you get your own answers. If you are receiving information which does not sound correct or comfortable to you, then listen to yourself and turn that other messenger off. Trust your own information and your own voice.

There are different aspects of you as spirit that relate to your body and the inner voice is where these various aspects of you communicate. The soul personality is the part of you that relates to the body; the entity, spirit or higher self (these terms are interchangeable) is the part of you that relates to the soul personality. Each is a part of the other, yet separate, to allow for creativity in the body. When you open communication between the part of you in your body and the part of you that is not, you allow for a flow of spiritual information that greatly enhances your experience in the body and your connection with God.

Learn to talk to yourself and you will learn to know many wonderful things about you. After all, who is more interesting to you than you? You will also know what is true for you, instead of what is true for others. You have all of your own answers and information so learn to ask yourself and listen. You do not have to receive or send communication if you do not wish. You have the God-given right to choose who and what you communicate with and about, so choose to talk to yourself about you more often. You will be amazed at what you know.

Our most important communication is with God. This is our source of light, love, power, validation and all things. At any time and place you can establish communication with God. You can use your fifth chakra for this communication to enhance your focus of energy. The sheer joy of communication is something we have all experienced at some time. This joy brings us closer to each other and to God.

Ground, be in the center of your head and run your earth and cosmic energies. Take time to do this.

Create and explode roses to help your energies run and to enhance your grounding.

Bring gold cosmic energy down through the top of your head and let it flow through the energy channels along your spine.

From the center of your head be aware of your fifth chakra at the cleft of your throat. Let the gold energy flow from the front to the back of your fifth chakra. Let the gold energy cleanse the chakra.

Be grounded and centered and create and explode roses for any foreign energy in your fifth chakra. Release the foreign energy down your grounding cord.

From neutral be aware of your inner voice. Let the gold energy cleanse this aspect of your fifth chakra. Ask yourself a question. Listen to the answer. Be sure the voice sounds like you.

Be grounded and create and explode roses. Allow any foreign energy in your inner voice to flow into a rose, and explode the rose. Let the foreign energy flow down your grounding cord.

Ask yourself another question and listen. If you do not like the answer, release your resistance to your own information down your grounding cord. You are your own best advisor and your strictest teacher.

Create and explode roses for limits to hearing yourself. Be amused about resisting yourself. Be still and listen to you.

Your most important communication is between you and yourself, and between you and your God. As you open and learn to control your fifth chakra, you can consciously put your attention on these two interactions. The meditation techniques help you focus on the chakra and learn to take control of it by cleansing it of lies and foreign energy. As you clear it, you are able to use it fully and for your spiritual purpose.

Communication is an aspect of love. Communication is something we as spirit enjoy more than most other things. In owning and using your fifth chakra you open to spiritual awareness in your communications. You are not limited to the body's ways of communicating. You open to the awareness of telepathy, clairaudience, pragmatic intuition, and the inner voice. They all bring you information and allow you to transmit information spiritually without the body limits.

Ground, be in the center of your head. Be aware of your earth and cosmic energies flowing through your system. Bring in a clear gold cosmic energy through your energy channels.

Tune in to your fifth chakra. Open your communication channels to God. Say hello. Allow yourself to receive a hello in return.

Create and explode roses for any beliefs that block you from talking with your God. Release down your grounding cord any energy that limits you in your personal relationship with your God.

Be still and allow yourself to have a quiet talk with your God.

Bring your energy to a comfortable place for you and your body. Bend forward and release energy.

Focus your meditations on communicating with yourself, your body, and your God. This will provide you with more information than you will be able to process and will help you stay on your path.

THE SEVENTH CHAKRA

The seventh chakra is located at the top of the head. This chakra has information about our ability to know and information about our trancemediumship. The seventh chakra is the most intricate chakra in the system. It is the place we as spirit are attached to the body. Ideally, we enter and leave the body through the seventh chakra. The seventh chakra is the master chakra of the seven major chakras.

Each of us is able to know whatever we need to know. We can access any information and the information on how to do this is located in the seventh or crown chakra. We do not store all of our information in this chakra; we store it in many places. The crown is the chakra we use to access all of our knowledge. We as spirit can focus our attention in this chakra and simply be still and know. We can know anything we wish to know. This ability assists us in our spiritual perspective because it transcends the intellect. Our intellect will limit us to the physical plane if we allow it.

The greatest temptation when opening this chakra is to play God. We may wish to lord it over others with our knowledge or use our knowledge for non-beneficial purposes. As we become aware of the power of knowledge, we may want to control others with our ability. Another temptation in opening this chakra is to want to share all you know with everyone. Your information may not be appropriate or meaningful for others. None of the abilities we have are meant to be used to control others. These abilities are meant to allow us to control our own energies and creations.

We can get out of touch with the physical reality if we allow ourselves to lose perspective in opening this chakra. The power gained is great and is most healing when used within one's own space. We need to first know ourselves and our God to use our knowledge most beneficially. It is not worth giving up ourselves as spirit for anything in the physical world, including knowledge.

Trancemediumship is another ability of the seventh chakra. Trance means an altered state of consciousness and medium means something through which a force acts. We can alter our energies (trance) to bring energy through our body (medium). The trancemedium ability is one we can use to alter our consciousness and bring spiritual energy through our physical body. Trancemediumship has our information on how to alter our energy so we can bring spiritual communication through our physical system.

There are many ways to use our trancemediumship. We can bring in our own energy, God's energy, another person's energy such as our mother's, or the energy of a being without a body. In most circumstances it is not appropriate or beneficial to bring energies other than your own through your body. Many people do bring in foreign energy and create a great deal of confusion in their lives. It is easy to recognize when someone is channeling foreign energy as the personality of the individual changes. Control of trancemediumship can be accomplished by grounding and meditating to identify and own one's unique vibration.

Channeling is a commonly known trancemedium practice. Trance channeling is the ability to leave one's body and allow another being to enter the body to communicate through it. Automatic writing and speaking in tongues are other trancemedium abilities. One needs to approach these uses of trancemediumship with caution. Some beings one brings in may not be beneficial to work with or may wish to take over the body.

Trancemediumship is such a high vibration of energy there are several traps one can fall into when opening and taking control of this skill. One is the misconception that one is special and better than others. We are each unique and the idea of being better than others leads into a competitive maze that blocks our unique beauty and spiritual growth. There is also the problem of dealing with this high vibration without losing control. When using one's trancemediumship for channeling another being, one needs to stay in charge to avoid a mishap; just as when one rides a very spirited horse, one needs to stay in charge to avoid a fall.

The flow of the high spiritual vibration into the lower vibration of the body requires training for the body. The body needs time and space to adjust and a plan for dealing with the energy. Also, if another being is involved, there needs to be an agreement as to how, when and for what purpose the body will be used. If one wishes to use trancemediumship to channel another being, it is essential to have someone as an energy control. This needs to be someone who loves you and will see that you and your body are safe. Otherwise the being may soon have greater control of the body than you do. You must remember that it is the original owner of the body who is responsible for the body's actions, regardless of what being is using it.

Trancemediumship is seldom validated for its use as a way to allow more of one's own spiritual vibration and information into the body. It is our ability to increase our vibration and allow spiritual communication through our body. It can be used to bring Christ-force energy into the body or to bring in your energy from a higher vibrational plane. We can also use this ability to bring in the energy of God. We can use our trancemediumship to experience the God within.

Ground from your first chakra to the center of the Earth. Be in the center of your head. Run your earth and cosmic energies.

Create and explode roses to help you ground, center and let the energy flow. Bring in a gold vibration of cosmic energy.

Bring your aura all around your body. Breathe deeply and relax. Be still and know yourself.

From the center of your head be aware of the crown of your head and your seventh chakra. Let the gold energy flow into the back of your seventh chakra and through your system to your first chakra, then up the front channels and out the front of your crown, cleansing your seventh chakra.

Create and explode roses to clear any foreign energy from your seventh chakra.

Bring your seventh chakra into present time. Release any past time energy down your grounding cord.

Be in the center of your head and be aware of your seventh chakra. Be still and know yourself as spirit. Know your spiritual purpose here on Earth. Know how you are or are not fulfilling your purpose.

Use your grounding to release energy. Clear energy by creating and exploding roses about your purpose.

Run your energies and bring your aura around you. Reinforce your grounding. Be in present time.

From the center of your head, be still and know you can communicate directly with God. Know your relationship with God.

Clear any interference by creating and exploding roses and releasing energy down your grounding cord. Own your seventh chakra and your ability to know.

By cleansing and owning your seventh chakra you open your ability to know. You can learn to know whatever you need to know at any time or place. You can use it to know your God and to know yourself. You can know your own answers. By owning your seventh chakra you have your power to create as spirit.

With your trancemedium abilities you can draw in more of yourself. You can increase your vibration to bring your spiritual energy more easily into your body. Use this ability to have more of yourself. Tune in to your inner voice to validate that it is you and not an energy you do not want. This ability is best left alone until all other aspects of your energy system are in your control. It is also recommended that you have a teacher or energy control if you plan to use this ability to relate to anything besides yourself and God. Before using your trancemediumship for channeling ask yourself, what other being do you want in your space when you have yourself and God?

Use your seventh chakra carefully and gently. There is great power in the seventh chakra. It is your connection between spirit and body. The seventh is where you experience revelation or the ability to reveal yourself to you. It contains your ability to know yourself and God, and to know God Within.

CHAKRA MEDITATION

The following guided meditations are presented to help you learn more about your chakras and the information you have stored in them. You can use all of the exercises during one meditation, or you can select ones most useful to you at the moment. You may find it helpful to focus more on one chakra than another if you have a lot happening in that area in the present. For example, if you are experiencing a great deal of emotional upheaval, it would be helpful to put your attention on learning to focus in the sixth chakra and cleansing the second chakra.

The meditations can help you learn to know yourself and get in touch with what you already know. They can also help you see what you are learning. Allow your meditation to be a process that leads you to yourself. Let your spiritual development be a journey, instead of trying to rush to a destination, and you will find a great deal of fun in your growth. Every meditation time can bring you to new insights and deeper spiritual awareness if you approach it with lightness and joy.

The meditations are divided into three segments and use the techniques presented earlier in the book as well as some new techniques. You will find it helpful to practice the earlier meditations to help you master the techniques. Relax and enjoy getting to know yourself.

Ground from your first chakra to the center of the Earth. Be in the center of your head. Run your earth energy up your leg channels to your first chakra and down your grounding cord.

Bring gold cosmic energy down through your seventh chakra through channels on each side of your spine all the way to your first chakra. Let the gold cosmic energy mix with your earth energy and flow up the channels along each side of your chakras till it fountains out the top of your head at your seventh chakra.

Let some of the energy flow from your fifth chakra at the cleft of your throat down your arms and out of your hand chakras.

Allow the gold energy to flow all around you through your aura. Be still a moment and experience the flow of energies.

From the center of your head, be aware of the gold energy flowing up the channels on each side of your chakras. Let the energy flow from the front to the back of your first chakra, flowing out the back and down your grounding cord.

Continue to let the energy flow up the channels and flow through the second chakra, filling it with gold energy and flowing out the back and down the grounding cord.

Let the energy continue to and through the third chakra and out the back and down the grounding cord.

As the gold energy flows to the fourth chakra, filling it from front to back with gold energy, let the energy leaving the back of the chakra flow up since it is now mostly cosmic energy.

Continue to let the energy flow to the fifth chakra, and fill it from front to back, and let it flow out the back of the fifth chakra. Let it flow up to the cosmos as it leaves your system.

Allow the flow of energy to go to the sixth chakra and fill it from front to back and flow out the back and up to the cosmos.

As the flow of gold energy continues, let it fountain out the top of your head at your seventh chakra. Let it fill your seventh with the gold energy and then flow up and out the top of the seventh and all around and through your aura.

Be grounded and in the center of your head. Be still and allow the flow of energy to cleanse and heal your chakras.

Allow time to enjoy and benefit from this cleansing.

This chakra cleansing exercise can be a central part of your meditations as you begin to tune in to your chakras. It is an effective general cleansing that can prepare you for whatever specific work you wish to do.

Ground, center and run your energies. Let the energy continue to flow through each chakra, and up and out the seventh chakra, and through your aura.

Take your hand and put it in front of your first chakra without touching your body. Feel the energy here. Be still and eventually you will experience the vibration of this energy center. Use your grounding to release any excess or unwanted energy.

Move your hand up to the second chakra just below your navel and feel the vibration there. Notice the difference from the first chakra. Use your grounding to release energy.

Continue to move your hand, bringing it up to the third chakra at the solar plexus, and feel that energy. Feel the difference in each chakra. Create and explode roses to release energy.

Put your hand down and let the gold cosmic energy flow through the chakra from front to back and cleanse the third chakra. Meditate on this flow of energy for a moment.

Again, put your hand in front of your third chakra and feel the energy. Notice if there is any difference in the energy flow or its vitality after consciously focusing energy there.

Slowly move your hand up to the fourth chakra near your heart, the fifth chakra at the cleft of your throat and the sixth chakra at your brow, feeling each one in turn without touching your body, so you can focus on feeling the energy in the chakra. Use your grounding to release energy. Allow time to feel each chakra.

Move your hand up to the top of your head and feel your seventh chakra and the energy flowing out the top of your head. Create and explode roses to release energy.

As you do this with each of the chakras in turn, you get a sense of the energy in each. Stay focused in the sixth chakra and stay grounded as you do this so you do not get confused. The sixth chakra is the neutral place for you to view your spiritual reality without judgement or fear.

You may feel warmth, coolness, tingling, blocks in the flow or other sensations. Let yourself meditate on the things you feel and learn to translate them into meaningful information for you. Hot may mean you are running too much energy in a chakra; cold usually means you are running too little energy. With this information you can make adjustments to your energy flow and balance your chakras.

You can also use your clairvoyance to read your aura and get information about your chakras. Since the aura is a projection of energy from each of the chakras, you can determine the state of a chakra by reading the corresponding aura layer. Read the first layer of your aura and you will know what is happening in the present in your first chakra.

Ground, be in the center of your head. Run your earth and cosmic energies. Activate your sixth chakra and use your clairvoyance.

Look at the first layer of your aura, which is the layer closest to your body. Translate the vibration to a color. Translate the color to a few words. Be aware of what this means to you about the state of your first chakra.

Use your grounding and energy flow to cleanse any dense or dark energy from your chakra and consequently from your aura. Run gold energy through the chakra to clear it.

Create and explode roses for any foreign energy or blockage in your aura and first chakra.

Bring the first layer of your aura and your first chakra into present time.

Look at each of the seven major layers of your aura one at a time and repeat the above exercises for each one.

Do this exercise slowly and take notes, and you will gain a great deal of information about your chakras. For example, you might see the first layer of your aura is bright clear green. You could translate this to growth and change. This would indicate that you are changing your relationship to the physical reality. This would explain your experience of a great many changes in your life. You might be changing your job, a relationship, where you live or other major shifts in your physical reality. If the energy had been dark, you would have known that you needed to cleanse foreign energy from the layer and the chakra.

By meditating on your chakras and cleansing and owning them, you gradually open and activate them. When you combine cleansing with activating, you have a smoother journey. Spend thirty minutes a day meditating on your chakras, and you will create a great deal of growth and spiritual awakening for yourself.

SPIRITUAL OPENING

The Christian Bible contains symbolic information about the spiritual awakening of man from Genesis to Revelation. The opening and use of the chakra system are detailed in the Book of Revelation in the New Testament of the Bible. In the Book of Revelation the chakras are referred to as churches, opening seals, candlesticks and other symbols. This Book was written in symbolic language to protect the information from being destroyed when it was written, and because people often taught in symbolic terms at that time in history. Those who taught the Christian mysteries were being persecuted and information was being destroyed. There is the historical information and the spiritual information. As you read it from a spiritual perspective, you see that the symbology teaches about the spiritual awakening of the individual soul and of humanity as a whole.

As spirit in a body we go through a process of revealing our divine nature to ourselves. We reveal what we need to know, when we need it. This process, or revelation, is depicted in detail in the Book of Revelation which contains a description of the spiritual awakening of man. The Book of Revelation contains the symbolic story of how to open and master the chakra system and other spiritual abilities. It is the "how to do it" book about spiritual awakening and development. It tells us how John and Jesus the Christ awakened their chakras and spiritualized their bodies. It tells us how we can do this. It also tells us of the awakening and coming of age of the human race, which is what we are experiencing in the present.

All of the great spiritual teachers unseal the chakra system to use the information they have stored there. By allowing a spiritual perspective and learning the purpose behind each experience, they each learned the purpose of their mission on Earth. Jesus learned that he came to the Earth to be the way or path for humankind to follow back to God. Jesus activated his chakras and all of his spiritual abilities and mastered them in order to fulfill his mission.

Other teachers have accomplished this also and left us their message. The well-known teachers, such as Buddha, Jesus, Moses, Mohammed, Lao Tsu, and Confucius, as well as the unknown teachers, learned their spiritual purpose and manifested their message in the physical world. The Book of Revelation is a description of John's spiritual awakening and his message about the Christ within each of us. It tells how each of us can manifest God within. It also describes the awakening of mankind. This awakening is happening now. It is up to us whether we create a joyful or a frightening experience.

We all have the information we need to develop spiritually. We can evolve to the level where we can experience revelation as Jesus did. We can learn to master the physical body and be senior as spirit. It is necessary to be consciously aware that we create our own reality and are responsible for our creations. We can become as personally responsible as Jesus was. Since he was responsible for his creations, he attained his spiritual goals. He then returned all he had gained to God. We can do this also.

All of the information in the Book of Revelation is valid in present time: it describes a way to live life now. By using meditation techniques we can spiritualize the body and experience harmony with ourselves and God. We can use simple techniques to learn how to use our spiritual abilities and reveal our spiritual selves.

We are spirit and we have created this planet and these physical bodies through which we can develop the spiritual maturity to reunite ourselves with God. Jesus freed himself and through meditation we can free ourselves also. We need to be like children in their ability to live in the present and remember how to enjoy our spiritual growing up process. By meditating and activating the chakras, we spiritualize our physical world and the revelation happens.

Opening the chakras is a necessary step in our spiritual progress. Each chakra has some aspect of our spiritual information. We have to learn how to access and use the information to function fully in this or any other reality. When we awaken the chakras, we rapidly grow in awareness. Each life experience can lead us to greater understanding once we operate as spirit.

In our spiritual awakening we unfold like a flower. As we open spiritually, we need to allow the process to happen, rather than forcing it to happen. Instead of expecting things to take place as we wish, we need to allow for the experiences that emerge with the opening of each energy center, according to what we have stored there. Activating the chakras is a process and a variety of lessons accompanies the opening of each chakra. When we relax and allow the development with patience, all we seek unfolds before us.

Since the opening of the chakras is a process, we do not need to open one at a time. We can move to one where we work awhile and then on to another. We can move around in the system activating and adjusting our chakras. This way we can stay in balance. If we activate one chakra completely before paying attention to another, we may get out of balance. We usually emphasize one chakra during each life, and continue to develop the others to balance our system.

The physical reality operates in time and space, so we need to allow time for our development. The body needs time to adjust to our spiritual changes. For every spiritual adjustment there is a corresponding body reaction. Some of the body reactions can be unpleasant or frightening so it is essential to allow time to move through the growth caused by unsealing the chakras.

It is important to release resistance as you open the chakras so you do not block your own growth. The opening of any of the chakras can cause physical pain if you resist the process. Pain causes fear and disturbance to the body. The spiritual techniques and perspective help us to let go of any resistance, pain, or fear and allow our growth and healing to take place.

You will need to sit quietly and experience your chakras to learn to know what you have in them. Sit in your meditative position and prepare yourself by using the meditation techniques. You need quiet time to get to know yourself. As you develop awareness of your chakras and your relationship with your body, you will also develop your communication with God. Keep your focus simple and it will work. When you start making things complicated, your body has taken charge and is trying to be intellectual about the spiritual process. Spirit is simple. God is simple. Simplicity is powerful.

The chakras hold your lessons and you "break the seal" to open each major focus of learning. You take lifetimes to master each chakra. Patience is an essential element in your learning process. When you get impatient, use the techniques to bring your attention back to your spiritual perspective. Patience will get you what you want. Impatience will lead you to some other focus and deflect you from your lesson. You need to learn to focus your attention to accomplish a goal.

As a child in school you knew the value of enjoying your lessons in order to learn easily. Your amusement is vital as you open these lesson plans called the chakras and discover your amazing creativity. Without your amusement you become serious, use effort, and the process slows to a stop. When you lose the pleasure of the experience, use the techniques to regain your amusement and your spiritual perspective.

Our spiritual perspective is essential if we wish to master the chakra system. We will get lost if we use physical limits and judge ourselves. Neutrality and amusement help us understand and accept the lessons we have created for ourselves. As spirit we can rise above the limits of the body and learn easily and with joy.

Each chakra is a world of experience and information focused on one aspect of spiritual manifestation on this planet. We have the ability to open each and discover what we have stored there. This information is what we are using to create. We can clear any pictures and concepts we no longer need or want. This is both traumatic and joyous, frightening and fulfilling. We may fluctuate from ecstasy to terror. We can complete the process in spite of the vastness of the mission. All things are possible when we operate as spirit.

We create lessons throughout life to allow the learning process. Our meditation on our chakras is part of the process. By learning to clear them consciously, using our spiritual perspective and our ability to manipulate energy, we take charge of our life. By living life we learn and grow. For most people this is not a time to be cloistered but a time to learn through living. To experience God within, it is necessary to live fully and with as much spiritual focus as possible. To experience God one must live what one knows of God.

By opening your chakras you learn your way of manifesting your God-self. You learn how you best manifest in the physical reality, how you constructively relate to yourself and others, how you can use your will to serve God. You learn how to use your power, how to love and be loved, how to communicate spiritually and physically. You learn how to see clearly as a spiritual being and how to access the vast knowledge available to you. You remember how to relate to yourself as spirit and to all other spirit both within and outside of bodies. You learn who you are and how to go about accomplishing your spiritual goals.

You learn to balance your chakras so you have a balanced system. This balance is necessary to fully manifest the God within. You may have spent lifetimes focused on love and affinity at the expense of truth and light. You will need to learn about light and truth to balance. Most people learn about one or two things and then in later lifetimes balance the two. If you have sacrificed one thing for another, you are out of balance and will need to bring the lost aspect back to yourself.

Often balance is associated with the male and female vibrations. This is also called the yin and yang. The male and female aspects of each soul have to be brought into balance for the God within to be born. Our female and male aspects are manifest throughout our entire spiritual and physical systems, from the chakras to the cells. The male and female aspects of self can be seen clearly in the sixth and fourth chakras. The light and truth represent the male and the love and affinity represent the female. When both aspects of self are fully manifested throughout the system, the soul is in balance.

Many people depend on someone outside themselves to balance these male and female aspects. Often a husband and wife will each be very male and very female. To develop spiritually they will need to learn from each other and learn to balance the male-female aspects within themselves. Until they do, they are dependent on each other and not free to allow the God within as their true love.

Often the references to husband and wife in the Christian Bible relate to this male-female aspect within each of us. As we learn to have and balance both, we blossom like a flower to God. The references to the wedding and to marriage are to the balance of the male and female within each soul. As we balance these, we are truly creators. As we allow and balance our fourth and sixth chakras, we learn to have light and love. We begin to live what we know of God.

By unsealing the chakras we learn where we are in balance and where we are out of balance. The development of the sixth chakra brings us clear seeing to have the truth and the light. The development of the fourth chakra brings us love and oneness. The seventh chakra lets us know God and the first has the information about how to live our experience and awareness of God. The second chakra gives us strength of will, the third our power and energy, and the fifth the joy of communication. With the knowledge we have in our chakras, we can learn to manifest what we know of God. By grounding in this reality and clearing any interference to manifesting ourselves as spirit, we create what we are meant to be: children of God.

Seven Wheels

Seven wheels
Seven wheels
Turn and heal
Turn and heal
Seven wheels
Seven wheels
Turn and heal

The first wheel tells us
How to live on Earth
It tells the story
Life death and birth

If you want to know
How another man feels
Or how you feel yourself
It's the second wheel

The third wheel turns
Like a mighty furnace
Turn it on up
Ain't nobody can burn us

The fourth wheel tells us
how to be at one
Turn it for yourself
And you'll have more fun

With the fifth wheel listen
Everything is heard
Clean it on out
And then spread the word

With the sixth wheel open
You can watch and see
Clean out the lies
Truth will set you free

The seventh wheel tells us
What we need to know
Be still and Listen
Let the story unfold

Seven wheels a-turnin'
You're the charioteer
Jesus left a road-map
and you need not fear

For the God almighty
Is on your side
Just ground and center
And enjoy the ride

Bill Broomall

Index

Church of Divine Man
CDM Psychic Institute
2402 Summit Ave.
Everett, WA 98201
(206) 258-1449

Branch Locations

Bellingham CDM
1311 "I" St.
Bellingham, WA 98225
(206) 671-4291

Spokane CDM
N 2803 Lincoln
Spokane, WA 99205
(509) 325-5771

Portland CDM
3314 SW First Ave.
Portland, OR 97201
(503) 228-0740

Tacoma CDM
4604 N 38th
Tacoma, WA 98407
(206) 759-7460

Seattle CDM
2007 NW 61st St.
Seattle, WA 98107
(206) 782-3617

Vancouver CDM
P.O. Box 80412
Vancouver, BC V5H 3X6
(604) 688-9985

If you are interested in learning more about meditation, healing, clairvoyance, and chakras, contact the Church of Divine Man/CDM Psychic Institute, or one of its Branches, for information.

☐ MEDITATION *Key to Spiritual Awakening*
by Mary Ellen Flora
Seven spiritual techniques that can lead you to yourself. $7.95 per book
☐ HEALING *Key to Spiritual Balance*
by Mary Ellen Flora
Get back in touch with your unique healing energies. $7.95 per book
☐ CLAIRVOYANCE *Key to Spiritual Perspective*
by Mary Ellen Flora
Techniques to help develop your clairvoyant abilities. $10.00 per book
☐ CHAKRAS *Key to Spiritual Opening*
by Mary Ellen Flora.
Get a copy for a friend! $10.00 per book
☐ I BELIEVE *Sermons*
by M. F. Slusher
Each of us is spirit and a part of God. $15.00 per book
☐ *The Inner Voice*
A periodic newsletter on spiritual awareness. A donation is appreciated.

CASSETTE TAPES:

☐ MEDITATION *Key to Spiritual Awakening*
Meditation techniques and a guided meditation. $9.95 per one-hour tape.
☐ HEALING *Key to Spiritual Balance*
Guided healing exercises and techniques. $9.95 per one-hour tape.
☐ CHAKRAS *Key to Spiritual Opening*
A guided chakra meditation. $9.95 per one-hour tape.

CDM Publications
2402 Summit Ave. Everett WA 98201

Please send me the items I have checked above. I am enclosing $_____ (please include $1.50 per item for postage and handling). Washington state residents add 7.9% sales tax. Send check or money order--no cash or COD's please. *Please allow six weeks for delivery. Prices and availability subject to change without notice.*

_____

name

_____

address

_____

city   state   zip

As a spiritual teacher, Mary Ellen Flora has helped thousands of people become more spiritually aware. She has dedicated her life to teaching others that they are spirit and a part of God, and teaching techniques to assist them in their spiritual awakening.

Mary Ellen's commitment to spiritual teaching led to the creation and growth of the Church of Divine Man and its teaching arm, the CDM Psychic Institute, in the Pacific Northwest. She co-founded the Church in 1976 with her husband, M. F. "Doc" Slusher. The Church's purpose is "to teach and to serve spiritual evolvement through our faith and practice."